#BAHRAIN

First Hand Accounts
of the Evolving Crisis

By Lars Hume

ISBN: 1482594307
ISBN-13: 9781482594300
Library of Congress Control Number: 2013903571

CreateSpace Independent Publishing Platform
North Charleston, South Carolina

received a call around lunchtime today from my Bahraini Shi'a friend Ali asking me if I wanted to attend a Shi'a Ashoura procession in his local village. Ashoura is the Shi'a festival of mourning for the martyrdom of Hussein, the grandson of the Prophet. I've always wanted to see an Ashoura procession in person and readily agreed to meet him right after work. I didn't have time to change my clothes before we met, but luckily I was already mostly dressed in black (as everyone else was), even though my outfit was a bit more formal than I would have preferred. We scrambled to find parking and then quickly walked through the streets to find a good place to watch. Ali greeted many people along the way. As a Western man, despite my brown hair, I clearly was an outsider. I watched as the parade of marchers made their way through the streets. There were people dressed up, re-enacting the slaying of their religious hero Hussein, and the subsequent abuse of the women and children. There were men dressed up as Sunni warriors carrying long pikes topped with heads made of plaster representing the Shi'a martyrs who had died along with Hussein.

Several times, Ali wanted to move to a new area to get a better view, so we marched along with the crowd as they swayed back and forth and pounded their chests in a strong, rhythmic pattern. I received long looks and double takes as people must have wondered for a moment what I was doing there. There was one group who had small chain whips, and they would whip their backs after each slow step, suggesting their willingness to suffer with Hussein. Periodically, small groups would pass who would be fiercely chanting and slowly raising their arms over their heads and then quickly slam their fists against their chest. It was the most intense cultural experience of my life.

I moved to Bahrain a few months after the Shi'a demonstrators were forcibly removed from the Pearl Roundabout. In the fall of 2011, I regularly heard propane tanks detonated in the distance, saw smoke off in the horizon, and passed groups of policeman in body armor standing at the entrances to Shi'a neighborhoods, waiting for a challenge. I even occasionally caught whiffs of tear gas and saw masked demonstrators obstruct roads. The unrest continued and changed from month to month as both sides responded to the moves of the others.

Bahrain is a key battleground in what I call the Sunni-Shi'a "Cold War." It is like the Berlin of the US-USSR Cold War period. The Sunni side is led by Saudi Arabia, battling Iranian influence throughout the region. This is playing out in Syria, Iraq, Lebanon, and other countries. In Bahrain, the level of Iranian influence is debated, but nobody doubts that Iran is at least giving encouragement and diplomatic support to the Bahraini Shi'a opposition.

The majority Shi'a population in Bahrain is ruled by a Sunni King. Shi'a are estimated at around 65 percent, and the Sunnis at about 35 percent, of the citizens of Bahrain. Residents from other countries, especially India, Philippines, and Pakistan, make up about half of the population. The Bahraini Shi'a have complained about discrimination in housing and jobs (including in the government and military), gerrymandering of the voting districts, and rapid naturalization of Sunni residents, among other social grievances. However, the core problem seems to be the unelected prime minister, the king's uncle, who has been in office for over forty years. Additionally, the upper house of parliament, the *Majlis al-Shura,* is solely appointed by the king, and it has veto power over the laws passed by the lower house, the Council of Representatives.

After the government forced the demonstrators out of the Pearl Roundabout, it badly mishandled the situation. They allowed many people, including those in government jobs, to be fired for participating in the demonstrations. They decided that it was the right time to destroy Shi'a mosques that had been built without a permit. They minimized the opposition's demands as merely being an Iranian plot to take over the country. They also accused hospital employees of denying services to Sunnis and helping people fake injuries during the unrest. There were numerous reports of government abuses, including torture of detained protestors. With the leaders of most of the Shi'a opposition groups in prison, there was an initial pause in anti-government activity as people waited for news about whether they would be convicted or quickly released as part of an agreement.

To the Bahrain government's credit, they established the Bahrain Independent Commission of Inquiry, which was praised by outsiders as having been given wide authority and access to investigate the unrest and related abuses. Attempts at reconciliation have failed. The government organized a "National Dialogue" that addressed many fringe problems in Bahrain such as traffic and education, but did not come close to addressing the underlying grievances of the Shi'a opposition. Groups representing many different causes and interests were merely given two minutes to make a statement, and then a report was written up summarizing the views.

Social media has played a significant role in allowing groups to organize locally and communicate with the outside world. It affects international opinion, especially because the foreign press in Bahrain is heavily restricted. Social media is also driving sectarian conflict by allowing people to anonymously yell at each other. The impetus for this book is my fascination with seeing how far apart the two sides are, as seen through the window of their online posts.

Since I arrived, the unrest has taken many different forms, all in an effort to put pressure on the government to reform. For a few weeks, there were vehicle protests, where the opposition would tell everyone to drive to a certain place at a certain time to shutdown traffic in the area. Then protestors would throw oil on the roads, which caused a few accidents. They locked chains across major roads to cause traffic jams, and threw paint on police vehicles when they ventured into Shi'a neighborhoods. Then they organized a protest in the City Centre mall, with a hundred or so women marching and chanting. They tried to copy the Occupy movement started in America, by initiating the short-lived Occupy Budaiyah Highway protest. Protestors used Molotov cocktails with increasing frequency, and the police and military responded with massive amounts of tear gas. Burning roadblocks, especially made of tires, became more common. Then, some activists planted improvised explosive devices (IEDs) to attack the police, who responded with force. This was followed by the frequent use of hoax IEDs.

In the early days of the demonstrations at the Pearl Roundabout, the government waffled about what course to take. Press reports indicated the US government was putting pressure on the Bahraini government not to go down the Gaddafi path, making it clear that our continued support was contingent on them handling the demonstrations with non-lethal force. There seemed to be pressure from the Saudis not to go the Mubarak way: standing idle while the popular revolution gained strength. Saudi Arabia was upset at how Mubarak had been abandoned by the US government and was determined not to let the Bahrainis make the same mistake of letting the demonstrators take action unopposed.

The Bahraini government hesitated and let protestors occupy the Roundabout while Crown Prince Salman bin Hamad bin Isa Al Khalifa was given authority to try to negotiate. Protestors' demands changed from calls for limited reform, to eventually calling for an end to the regime. This made it difficult for many Sunnis to consider concessions to the Shi'a and weakened the main opposition group's position. The day after US Secretary of Defense Gates left Saudi Arabia, the Saudis sent hundreds of troops into Bahrain. This naturally created the impression that the US had approved the move. This led to fiery rhetoric between the Saudis and Iran. This could have been a factor in the alleged plots against Saudi diplomats in the United States and later in Bahrain.

During Ashoura, people expected the large groups gathering to celebrate would lead to increased demonstrations. The government had checkpoints throughout the country to prevent Shi'a demonstrators gathering in large numbers. Every time a significant demonstration broke out, they would close all the roads into the area in order to prevent other Shi'a from joining in.

Over time, the Sunnis began to get frustrated with the Shi'a demonstrations and the disruption the protests were posing to their lives. In Muharraq, a mixed Sunni-Shi'a area, a group of Sunnis threw rocks and bricks at Shi'a in a religious procession. This sparked fears of sectarian conflict. Sunnis also increased their calls on the government to take action against the Shi'a. The government did not allow most policemen to carry live ammunition. They were limited to tear gas, stun grenades, and possibly rubber bullets, though these were used less frequently. They eventually used "bird shot" which wounded, but only caused a few deaths. This allowed Bahrain to avoid a rising death toll and the resulting cycle of mass funeral gatherings/follow-up processions. To some Sunnis though, this relatively softer approach was not sufficient to deal with the problem.

Having lived in a variety of countries with ethnic disputes, I've seen how group identities and the associated security dilemmas can overshadow practical solutions that require people to trust the intentions of a group with a history of mistreating your people. After the demonstrations in February and March, it was common to hear people in Bahrain say that things would never be the same again, that the trust between the two communities was broken. Stores were boycotted based on the sect of the shop owner.

Is it conceivable that the king would "fire" his uncle, and the many other members of his family associated with the prime minister's office? A professor I had, Mr. Dowdle, once told me a regime's legitimacy is inversely proportional to the number and the size of pictures of the leader seen on the streets of the country. Bahrain is plastered with massive murals of the king, crown prince and prime minister. In a very odd attempt at public relations, there are many posters exclaiming the universal support the people have for the prime minister, including my favorite: "Khalifa, all of us love/prefer you."

Legitimacy is granted by the people. Monarchies are fine as long as that is what the people want. When the majority of the people no longer accept the system of government, change is inevitable. To a citizen of a Western country, the Shi'a demands for greater representation seem just. However, some Shi'a have at times shown such an allegiance to Iran that it is natural for the Sunnis to be wary of conceding more power to them. The underlying problem is a breakdown in trust that only grows worse as the conflict continues, and the future remains uncertain.

Will the government overreact, leading to a rising death toll, and an international perception that the regime needs to go? Will elements in the Sunni community get so frustrated with the situation that they take direct action against the Shi'a demonstrators, leading to sectarian conflict? Will the government make a deal with the main opposition group, Al-Wefaq, which may be rejected by hard-line elements in both the Shi'a and Sunni communities? Is there a way to protect the future of the Al Khalifa rule, and allay the fears of the Sunnis, while still meeting the demands for a more democratic government not dominated by the ruling family?

History of the Conflict

The schism within Islam into Sunni and Shi'a sects dates back to the seventh century-dispute concerning political and religious control of the Islamic community. The struggle continues today, with the Shi'a populations in the Arabian Peninsula struggling to obtain what they consider a more equitable form of government from the Sunni regimes that rule their countries. The shape and force of the Shi'a opposition has been a function of actions by their governments and events in the region.

Recent events have re-enforced the perception that the Shi'a are a rising force in the region. First among these events is the prominence of the Shi'a in the new Iraqi government. The recent rise to power of the Shi'a after years of abuse under Saddam Hussein's regime gives hope to other Shi'a populations. Secondly, the election of President Ahmadinejad in Iran, in combination with a checkered US effort in Iraq, has led to an emboldened Iranian foreign policy and contributed in some degree to a sense of a stronger Shi'a force in the region. Lastly, Hezbollah's perceived victory against Israel in the summer of 2006 has strengthened the Shi'a position within Lebanon, as well as in the region generally, as Hezbollah touts the notion that the Shi'a militia is the only group to successfully challenge Israel.

Shi'a opposition movements in the Arabian Peninsula had, prior to the Iranian revolution, generally limited their calls for reform to specific improvements in their social and religious lives. The Iranian revolution gave them the confidence and ideological and material support to push for sweeping changes to the current regimes. Small numbers of individuals in Kuwait, Bahrain, and Saudi Arabia planned violent anti-regime attacks in the early 1980s. Since the late 1980s, Iran has generally softened its rhetoric, and while demonstrations have at times turned violent, the majority of the Shi'a opposition has advocated change through peaceful methods.

The successes of the Shi'a in Iraq, Iran, and Lebanon have affected Shi'a opposition groups in the Arabian Peninsula and the responses of their Sunni rulers. Immediately after the US-led invasion of Iraq some Gulf leaders allowed more freedom in Shi'a religious rites. Although the situation varies within each country, a general rising expectation of reform has occurred among the Shi'a in the Arabian Peninsula. The degree to which the Sunni regimes in the Gulf can accommodate these rising expectations will largely determine the direction and intensity of the Shi'a opposition. These rising expectations dramatically increased after the Arab Spring swept the region.

The Shi'a opposition groups are not openly anti-Western and would not necessarily adopt a negative policy towards Western interests. Other than in Bahrain, the Shi'a are a minority within their countries. As a result, they are very unlikely to ever obtain control of the countries where they reside through democratic means.

In the case of Bahrain, democratic reform could eventually lead to a Shi'a- controlled government. Would a Shi'a-controlled Bahraini government be as pro-West as the Al Khalifa regime? The answer is almost certainly in the negative. Shi'a protests over the years and comments from Bahraini Shi'a religious leaders suggest that a primarily Shi'a-led Bahraini government would face pressure to distance itself from its current close relationship with the United States and other Western states. However, there are a number of factors that could act to mitigate this pressure. Even though a Shi'a-dominated government might seek better relations with Iran, it might still feel sufficient threat from Iran that it would, like the Khalifas, find an alliance with the United States in Bahrain's interest. It might well also feel a need for the counterbalance against its other big neighbors—Saudi Arabia and Iraq—that good relations with the United States or another outside power would provide. A major determinant affecting US-Bahraini relations in the event of a Shi'a-led government would be the US stance regarding the change and the instability that would occur in making the transition.

A Brief History of the Shi'a Opposition in Bahrain

There has been a sizeable Shi'a community in Bahrain since the early Islamic period. The community was strengthened by Iran's adoption of Shi'a Islam as a state religion under the Safavids, who began ruling Bahrain in 1602. Safavid rule allowed the Shi'a to set up centers of clerical study that emerged as some of the most prominent in the Arab world.[i] Shi'a control of Bahrain came to an abrupt end in 1782, when the Al Khalifa tribe from Qatar conquered the island.[ii]

In Bahrain, approximately 60 to 70 percent of the population are Shi'a, which makes it the only country in the Gulf where the Shi'a are a majority.[iii] Historically, they have been kept out of the ruling bodies of government. This political disenfranchisement has been the primary source of discontent among the Shi'a and has led to varying degrees of instability during the past two hundred years.

With the help of British advisors, the royal family was able to consolidate its rule in the 1930s and 1940s, through a series of reforms and improvements to the infrastructure, including extending the road system and building bridges between the two major islands.[iv] The discovery of oil on the main island during this period—and the resulting employment opportunities—offset the potential for labor unrest due to the drastic downturn in the pearl industry. Most of the Shi'a protests during this period were in response to specific incidents rather than an expression of general opposition to the regime. For example, in 1934 and 1935, there were protests aimed at improving the court system in response to harsh sentences given to the Shi'a.[v] Other protests focused on improving work conditions and compensation.

This trend began to change in the 1950s. According to author John Duke Anthony, "The first significant manifestation of popular agitation during that decade occurred in 1954, when local leaders, including spokesmen for the Sunni and Shi'a religious sects, successfully organized committees, demonstrations, and a general strike in support of sweeping reforms."[vi] In response to these actions, the amir allowed elected councils to deal with education and public health matters. These changes proved insufficient, and in 1956 (during the period of the Suez Crisis), riots broke out and threats were made to the amir's life. A state of emergency was declared; British troops were called upon to restore order; and the opposition leaders were imprisoned.[vii]

Throughout the 1960s, the Shi'a continued to agitate for free speech, press, and assembly. They protested the ban on political parties as well as the general political climate that had the effect of forcing any individual or group calling for reforms to organize outside of Bahrain.[viii] Periods of intense demonstrations were usually met with offers of minor reforms, which were then usually only partially implemented. In the 1960s, the demonstrations were less focused on the tension between Shi'a and Sunni due to the threat felt from Iran's territorial claims to Bahrain.[ix] When Iran finally renounced its claim in 1970, the Shi'a-specific aspect of their protests slowly began to re-emerge.

In the early 1970s, Amir Isa attempted to make some dramatic reforms to the political system in Bahrain. He decreed in June 1972 that there would be elections for a constituent assembly to debate and approve a draft constitution.[x] Many Shi'a applauded this measure. However, the fact that the amir would be appointing twenty-three of the forty-five members of the assembly suggested that he was not prepared for a dramatic change to the political system. The principal reform was the creation of a thirty-member National Assembly to serve as the main lawmaking body. The elections held in 1973 had a very high voter turnout. The Amir was accused of gerrymandering the electoral districts to ensure an outcome favorable to his interests.[xi]

The wide range of political candidates elected showed that the population was not as revolutionary as the regime had supposed. It did show that Shi'a voters almost exclusively voted for other Shi'a, and that Arab Shi'a voted for other Arab Shi'a (over Persian Shi'a candidates).[xii] These reforms alleviated some of the anti-regime sentiment; however, a significant portion of the population still felt that additional changes were needed.

Iranian Support to the Shi'a Opposition

The underlying discontent among Bahraini Shi'a was further fueled by the Islamic Revolution in Iran. Ayatollah Khomeini called for the overthrow of the Al Khalifa regime, and his Islamic Revolutionary Guards Corps (IRGC) gave support to Bahraini Shi'a toward this end. These calls led to an assassination attempt on Amir Hamad in 1981. Following this attempt, a wide crackdown on Shi'a led to the arrest and deportation of many Shi'a considered to be engaged in anti-regime activities. Iran continued to back Bahraini Shi'a oppositionists, such as Hadi Mudarissi's Islamic Front for the Liberation of Bahrain (IFLB), and the Bahraini wing of the Dawa (Islamic Call) Party.

Iran's unsuccessful attempt to export the revolution increased regime repression of the Shi'a. Iranian leadership became dissatisfied with the IFLB because of its unwillingness to accept Iranian direction. By the late 1980s, Tehran moved away from the IFLB and sought to improve relations with the Al Khalifa regime. The mid to late 1990s brought a widespread Shi'a uprising. There was a lot of the same street violence that we see today. There was even a group the government accused of being Bahraini Hezbollah whom they said received training and support from their big brothers in Lebanon.

Eventually, enough people were arrested and exiled that the violence leveled out by 1998.

When Sheikh Hamad assumed the throne in 1999, he announced a number of reforms that would increase Shi'a participation in the government. Important among them was the establishment of a representative lower house of parliament chosen through free elections. Among other reforms, the new amir granted amnesty to political prisoners and exiles, and abolished the "State Security Law" which allowed the government to hold individuals for up to three years without trial.[xiii] In 2000, he appointed a group to write a National Action Charter, laying out several reforms and making Bahrain a constitutional monarchy. The draft charter was approved by a referendum in 2001, and in 2002 Hamad proclaimed himself king with the declared legitimacy of the public's approval of the new constitutional system. Frederic Wheyrey explained, "By 2002, however, these promised reforms had either stalled or evaporated, fueling new levels of cynicism and resentment. Moreover, the emir, having designated himself king, unilaterally revised the 1973 constitution, subordinating the elected parliament to an appointed Majlis al-Shura and depriving the parliament of the ability to formally introduce new legislation or exert financial oversight over government ministries."[xiv]

In the 2000s there was steady pressure against the current system of government. The Shi'a opposition decided to boycott the 2002 elections and pressure the government for change outside the system. When, in 2004, the main opposition group Al-Wefaq decided to participate in the next elections in 2006, a significant group opposed the decision and split to form the Haq (Truth) Movement. In 2006, many Shi'a participated in the election and won nineteen of the forty seats. They tried to show that they could bring the change the Shi'a sought by working within the system. Over the next few years, however, they were not able to show any significant results from participating in the system. Protests and demonstrations continued at a steady pace, and moreover, expectations continued to rise. The Arab Spring set fire to the underlying resentment of the Shi'a people.

The planned demonstration for 14 February 2011 initially was focused on limited demands like an "end to corruption," and reform of the voting system. When a critical mass formed and stayed for days on end, their demands slowly grew. Suddenly speakers were calling for a complete end to the Al Khalifa regime. The festival-like atmosphere at the Pearl Roundabout continued for several days as two or three hundred thousand people congregated. Efforts by Crown Prince Salman to negotiate eventually stalled. Patience wore thin as some protesters moved to the Financial Harbor and other areas of Manama. Several hundred Saudi and UAE troops arrived as a sign of support, and the Bahrain security services used force to clear the Pearl Roundabout. They tore the Pearl monument down and put up barbed wire and stationed armored vehicles to block any return. The government arrested the hard-line leaders, and a new group called the 14 February Youth Alliance was formed. They seemed to be a loosely organized movement that followed the thinking of the detained hard line leaders. Over the next two years, the 14 February Youth Alliance and the mainstream Al-Wefaq would compete for the hearts of the people, using different tactics to achieve different objectives.

15 JANUARY 2012

Bambina (@bambinabrn)
There was a time to forgive and forget, followed by forgive and don't forget, now we shall never forgive never forget #bahrain

Tonight I drove along Budaiyah Highway with my son. He was really impressed with the body armor of the approximately eight policemen standing across the street from Bani Jamra, looking like they were expecting something to happen. Along the way, we also saw a dumpster turned over, trash spilling into the street. We pulled alongside a convoy of about seven police vehicles, which were driving slowly in the right lane. I joked about how we don't want to be hanging around these guys too long, and then they all moved into the left lane leaving me in the middle of their convoy for a few blocks. Social media sites showed a clip of police vehicles chasing, and nearly running over, presumably Shi'a young men in the village of Barbar (along Budaiyah Highway) earlier in the day.

17 JANUARY 2012

Nicholas Kristof (@NickKristof)
In #Bahrain, activist @NabeelRajab reaches a red line, says it's time for the king to step down:

THELADYINRED (@theladyispyon)
#Bahrain heavy attack on protesters now in the village of Barbar after procession of third day of funeral of martyr Salma Mohsin

S. Yousif Almuhafda (@SAIDYOUSIF)
#Bahrain the riot police are shooting us now with tear gas and sound graneds now and they are many injured #Arabspring

My wife phoned me yesterday morning while I was at work. "There is no denying that there was a huge explosion. It shook the house. It wasn't like a gas-can explosion; it was more like a military explosion. My heart is still racing. Can you find out and call me back? It was the same time as the other one. This one was huge and close." We live within a couple kilometers of a Bahrain Defense Force base; it is possible it came from there.

The king announced some reforms, such as allowing the parliament to approve the appointment of cabinet officials, and he promised to rebuild some of the mosques that were destroyed soon after the security forces dispersed the protesters last spring. The mosques (some of them small prayer rooms) were destroyed because they had been built without proper permits. I can't imagine who thought that was a good time to take that action, or how it was intended to help calm the situation or deter protestors. The king added, "Our people have proven their desire for continuing with reforms…We complete the march today with those who have an honest patriotic desire for more progress and reform. I must mention here that democracy is not just constitutional and legislative rules; it is a culture and practice and adhering by the law and respecting international human rights principles."

Sayyed Hadi al-Mosawi, a member of Wefaq, responded: "His speech fell short of our expectations…The measures did not reflect any of the opposition or the people's demands."

19 JANUARY 2012

Mohammed Ashoor (@mohdashoor)
Black smoke filling the sky of #Bahrain at the moment, and from all areas!!

S.Yousif Almuhafda (@SAIDYOUSIF)
#Bahrain tens of thousends are chanting now step down khalifa, they meant the priminster who is in power more than 40 years

I saw a video the other day that showed groups of young Shi'a in a nearby village in military formation. They were wearing burial shrouds, symbolic of their willingness to be martyrs for the cause. They awkwardly marched in a goose step, possibly inspired by the Soviets, Nazis, or other totalitarian regimes. Then they stuck their arm out straight out in some sort of salute. The camera then panned to a guy struggling to rappel down a three-story building, perhaps intending to show their ability to carry out paramilitary operations. The groups ended their march by raising a flag near a large (about ten-foot tall) mock-up of the Pearl Roundabout.

My family and I went to the Bahrain Airshow today. We saw about fifteen different fires along the way. Some of them were large with black plumes of smoke, in the distance. Others were visible from the highway. It seemed likely that they were intended to make it clear to the international visitors that the security situation in Bahrain was not under control.

Tonight Al-Wefaq hosted a large rally and parts of the crowd chanted that they wanted Khalifa to step down. The 14 February protests began with very limited demands and eventually turned to calls for an end to the "regime." After the firm response by the government, including life sentences to several leaders, the public calls have been moderated. One guy even thought it was important enough to explain that the crowd wasn't calling for an end to monarchy; they just wanted to the Prime Minister to step down.

20 JANUARY 2012

M. K. Al-Binateej (@ATEEKSTER)

Fight in Arad between Rioters & Patriots. Rioters threw rocks & Molotov fire bombs at civilians in the shopping area. #Bahrain

Sayed Hassan (@WLEXT)

#Sar is a war zone, literally, police sirens, protesters honking & shouting, mercanaries shooting tear gas, ambulance was there too

We invited a couple of families over to our house for dinner tonight. They called on their way to our house to say they wouldn't be able to make it, because traffic was at a standstill and there were a lot of police and demonstrators on the streets. One YouTube clip showed thousands of people marching in the street around the Burgerland Roundabout.

There is no doubt that the coming weeks are going to be dangerous. Both sides appear to have learned a lot from the mass demonstrations of last February and March and the ongoing protests of the past year. It is a war of attrition. The Sunni community gets more frustrated, increasing the odds of a sectarian conflict. The government is torn between a deal they will almost certainly be unable to make due to Saudi and royal family pressure, and their inability to contain the violence. So there is no deal, and things continue to escalate. The longer they wait to make a deal, the less likely it will be accepted by the Sunni community who trust the Shi'a less with each passing day. If the government uses force, as did Gaddafi and Assad, they will similarly become international pariahs. If they don't, the protestors have a chance of gaining a critical mass like they did in Egypt. The government has so far prevented the large-scale demonstrations from materializing. There seems to be a strong commitment for a return to the Pearl Roundabout leading up to February 14. Can they be stopped without brutal force?

22 JANUARY 2012

Mazen Mahdi (@MazenMahdi)
RT @vendettaBH صور من تكسير برادات جواد 24 ساعة http://yfrog.com/esfuhfwj #Bahrain Thugs in busaiteen attacked jawad 24hr coldstore!

M. K. Al-Binateej (@ATEEKSTER)
Wefaq is desperate for "martyrs" & they plan to push their followers (especially women) on 24/1 to confront police. #Bahrain

Toby C. Jones (@tobycraigjones)
Still hard to understand US total radio silence on #Bahrain crackdown.

Albahraini (@alhojairy)
Mother of martyr Muwali:thanks God my son is martyr in heaven,I am proud of him & all martyrs, his martyrdom will bring us victory

On my way to see my son's game yesterday, I saw smoke rising from the area behind the building across the street from where the game was being held. I heard that some guys had blocked the road with burning tires. This and worse was happening in many areas in Bahrain. Molotov cocktails are increasingly common in some areas. We went to the Bahrain Mall on the edge of Sanabis yesterday. There were three policemen in body armor standing on the corner of each street leading into the area.

Over the weekend there was a funeral in Muharraq for a young Shi'a man who was found dead in the water in Amwaj. They say there was a skirmish, as local Sunnis did not want any demonstration activity anywhere near their area. The brawl was dispersed by the police, but it serves as further evidence that Sunni frustration is mounting. Following the incident, several shops and restaurants owned by both Sunni and Shi'a were attacked.

Leading Bahraini Shi'a cleric Isa Qassim surprised many people by taking a very strong stance against police violence directed at female protestors. There have been pictures and videos showing Shi'a women being arrested and treated in a way that made many Shi'a angry. He said that Shi'a were obligated to "crush" the police if they see this happening. Sheikh Qassim is very influential here and is known for encouraging non-violence, so this statement could really have an impact.

There is a lot of talk about 24 January being the day the Shi'a begin even more aggressive activities leading up to the 14 February anniversary. We'd better make our planned trip to the water park in the City Centre mall tomorrow while we still can.

24 JANUARY 2012

Sparrow (@iCameldos)
Clashes ongoing since afternoon, Rebels refusing to retreat and controlled many of their villages main roads #Bahrain #BahrainFist #14feb

Ali Al-Muharraqi (@Ali_Al-Muharraqi)
RT "@DouaaMahran Were sick and tired from bieng threatned by protesters , action must be taken ! #Bahrain !"

On my way to work this morning, I did a double take as I saw two military armored trucks with soldiers standing up in the turret with mounted machine guns. The military was out on the streets for a brief period in the early days after 14 February 2011 but have since left the policing to the police (Ministry of Interior). Perhaps they were just traveling to another base, but in light of the expected increase in violence today, I hope they weren't being called in to help contain the unrest. There were a few fires and smoke plumes visible about a third of a kilometer off the highway.

The US Embassy announced they were moving those embassy personnel who were located in the predominantly Shi'a-dominated area of Budaiyah Highway. Although this decision had likely been in the works for several weeks, announcing it at this time created the appearance that they were reacting to the recent Shi'a plans to step things up in the next few weeks. There was also a Travel Alert issued for US citizens to avoid coming to Bahrain.

I saw an ambulance with sirens blaring for the first time today. I've heard in the press that Shi'a fear they will be arrested if they go to the hospital. There were triple the number of police at the entrance to certain Shi'a neighborhoods. I took my son to a youth activity tonight as usual. Social media showed very intense skirmishes with groups of Shi'a in villages like Sanabis and Diraz wildly throwing rocks and Molotov cocktails at police. Police were holding their ground, apparently careful not to be divided and drawn into more dangerous situations. I'll found out tomorrow just how bad things were tonight.

26 JANUARY 2012

Meena (@MeenaSabah)
I have passed by 6 villages and they were under excessive use of #tear-gas used by AlKhalifa regime in #Bahrain.

samiraalsalem (@samira117164)
#Bahrain@Peace !!IF THE POLICE DO NOT USE SOME FORCE THE WAFAQ REGIME WILL TAKE CONTROL OF THE STREETS HURTING INNOCENTS!!!!@BAHRAIN

Yesterday my wife and children were driving to a computer class but didn't make it. There was a large demonstration in the diplomatic area causing traffic around most of the major highways. They eventually had to turn around because they would have missed the class.

Over thirty policemen were injured on the twenty-fourth. My friend in Saar said on the night of the twenty-fourth he heard gunshots (likely rubber bullets or batons) outside his compound walls for about five hours. Yesterday a man intentionally crashed his car into police cars and later died in the hospital, although some say he was in police custody. Three others also died. There were intense confrontations with police in many neighborhoods. This usually involved about twenty policemen standing and a group of twenty to two hundred people throwing rocks, rods, and sometimes Molotov cocktails. The police would fire tear gas or stun grenades. I heard a police station in Sitra was attacked with Molotov cocktails. I think if we see more attacks on government facilities the security services will respond much more forcefully. I called my friend Ali whom I haven't talked to in a couple weeks, to see how he was. He is a Shi'a from an area near Sanabis. He said it has been hard for him to leave and that the police are making it very difficult for them right now. He added that he has been staying inside for the most part.

On the way home from a restaurant tonight we passed through the Bilad al-Qadeem neighborhood. Traffic slowed as we saw about twenty policemen dealing with tires and other debris on fire, blocking the road heading in the other direction. Other policemen stood by keeping an eye on things.

28 JANUARY 2012

Aseel (@Aseel_Onm)
Obama administration using loophole to quietly sell arms package to #Bahrain | The Cable: http://bit.ly/wr6aNB

Ali came by our house yesterday for a visit. He talked a lot about how hard it is for him to move around with all the police activity. I asked him about the nationalities of the police officers and he said most of them were Saudis and Yemenis. (I don't think his perception is accurate.) I asked him about Pakistanis, and he said he agreed that there were also a lot of them too. He said the Saudis were the real problem, because their hatred for the Shi'a was the greatest. I suddenly noticed his legs were scraped and he had a fat lip. I asked him what happened. Between his broken English and my partial Arabic, he explained that he had an accident and fell. After I persisted in trying to understand better what had happened, he said he was hit by a car...a "crazy Saudi driver" hit him while he was walking in the road. I mentioned a couple of YouTube videos I had seen, and he said he doesn't view them because if he does he'll be thrown in jail. I showed him a couple. He saw one that had a title about police chasing demonstrators in their cars and really wanted me to watch that one. It showed the police narrowly missing someone who was running away. After he left, it occurred to me that perhaps his injuries were actually from some encounter with the police, but he didn't want me to clearly know that he was involved.

Tonight we heard explosions a couple of kilometers away. Most likely they were propane tanks the protestors had set on fire. Several videos showed large amounts of tear gas covering several square blocks in a variety of villages. There were a lot of complaints about tear gas in their homes and of reports of America agreeing to sell arms to Bahrain.

29 JANUARY 2012

MissScoutFinch (@MissScoutFinch)
#Wefaq statement today: "Attacks on women ... reflect the immoral behavior of non-national security forces" #Bahrain #racism

Al-Wefaq continues to run with the advice issued by their spiritual leader, Sheikh Isa Qassim, when he said to crush anyone who dishonors women after recent video clips showed women being arrested.

About forty-five minutes before my son's sports practice, we heard one of the streets near the field had a burning roadblock and that there was tear gas being used to disperse the demonstrators. I took another way to get there to avoid the roadblock. When I arrived, the coach was in the parking lot explaining that practice was canceled. He explained that while he was on the field, tear gas was blowing over the wall and was burning his eyes. His eyes were really red and a little swollen. On our way back, we saw one road that was blocked with wood pallets, dumpsters, and other random things. Another road had trash blocking the street.

4 FEBRUARY 2012

David Ferreira (@FourYawkeyWay)
No favorites. I condemn U.S. when it shields Bahrain & Israel from condemnation. I condemn China & Russia when it shields Assad.

Maximilian Forte (@1D4TW)

Now try passing a UNSC resolution against Bahrain, and let's see if the U.S. would sell out its ally/naval base (http://bit.ly/AqAPMo)

Sayed Yousif (@SayedYousif)

Banner "resisting &will never bow". Its totally true, everyone here confident that Pearl Sq 'll b recaptured. #Bahrain

The big story now is just how bad things will be next week. At work and church, from my landlord, neighbors, and parents at sports practice...I hear the same questions: What will the Shi'a do on 14 February? How committed are they to retaking the Pearl Roundabout? Will Wefaq (the main "moderate" group) also support that decision? Will things calm back down after 14 February? Last year, the government learned the lesson that force works, and it will definitely take strong measures to prevent another mass gathering. Can they control the crowds without looking like Assad in Syria? I think it is going to be a bloody day. Demonstrations and skirmishes continued this week, but I think they were mild compared to what will take place next week.

There are press reports about US Congressional opposition to selling weapons to Bahrain, even if those weapons are intended for external defense. Russia and China just vetoed UN action against Syria, and many people are comparing the hypocrisy of the US leading action against Syria while openly supporting Bahrain. When the government of Bahrain has to resort to greater force next week, it is going to put the US in a difficult position. If they don't use enough force, they could go down like Egypt. If they use too much, they will become Gaddafi and Assad and will face stronger international criticism and calls for significant reforms in the government.

6 FEBRUARY 2012

S. Yousif Almuhafda (@SAIDYOUSIF)

#Bahrain. : The health of Martyr Ali Al-haykii deteriorated after inhaling toxic gases, he stayed in SMC for a week until he died today"

Om Mohammed (@AmyBH2)
8 days left till the #lulureturn, make a choice of being killed & ur children at ur house by toxic gas or making a difference #bahrain

M. K. Al-Binateej (@ATEEKSTER)
Protests today in front of the iranian embassy at 4pm condemning iran's support for Assad & the coup plotters in #Bahrain

Ahmed (@ahmedalghattam)
Video that's shows the inhumane attacks on the police by Hezbolla Terrorists (#Alwefaq) blessed by HR orgs - http://youtu.be/_O6oTsm79M0 #Bahrain

These statements show the divide between the two groups. Many of the Sunnis see the Shi'a demonstrators as Hezbollah terrorists trying to take over the government for Iran. There has been a lot of discussion about the role of Twitter and Facebook in spurring the Arab Spring along. Besides the obvious role it plays in helping groups communicate and organize, it also exposes the various factions to the negative aspersions of the other groups.

A large group of Shi'a has been "occupying" an area in Meqsha near the Burgerland Roundabout, off of Budaiyah Highway, a couple kilometers from where the old Pearl Roundabout was. They are calling it Freedom Square. I think they are going to use it as a staging point to march towards the Pearl Roundabout on 14 February. I expect the police will try to disperse the crowd before 14 February.

There are still daily demonstrations, many of which are confronted by police with tear gas and stun grenades. They seem to be using some form of rubber bullets more frequently. I think the intensity of the demonstrations will build in a few days leading up to all sorts of chaos on the fourteenth.

8 FEBRUARY 2012

Kristen Chick (@kristenchick)
Bahrain says it denied journos visas bc so many were coming and it wanted to make sure we all got interviews w key figures. How kind.

Resistant (@Satraawi)
New photos: #US #marines of 5th fleet enjoying time w/ mercenaries of #Bahrain & claim they want #democracy for #syria!

The ongoing demonstration at Meqsha continues. The government seems to have extended their approval for the rally to continue through February 11. I'm sure the government will try to break it up before the fourteenth. Several of the speakers have encouraged the group of several thousand to join in the effort to retake the Pearl Roundabout.

The Bahraini government is being widely criticized for denying so many visas for journalists who want to cover the 14 February anniversary. I don't blame them for wanting to limit the coverage because it will no doubt be an ugly day, and they don't want to look like Assad and other dictators who cling to power against the people. However, the other side of the coin is when you restrict the flow of information, you really look like you have something to hide, and with today's media (including social media) there is no way the government will be able to stop the world from seeing.

Yesterday some photos were posted, allegedly depicting a Bahraini policeman with US Marines. They say the phone was dropped by a Bahraini policeman when he was running from a group of angry Shi'a trying to attack him. A Shi'a group is using the photos as proof that the US Marines are training the Bahraini police. In the press it says that Bahrain sends people on assignments to help secure a base in Afghanistan. Too bad this will give ammunition to those trying to portray the US as against the Shi'a cause.

Everyone seems to be making preparations for the fourteenth. At work, we talked about how our schedules would be affected, what was expected of us during that time, and lessons we learned from last year. At church last week, I explained to everyone our communication plan to inform people if we were going adjust the schedule because of unrest, and we discussed ways they should be prepared. It is hard to have that discussion without getting some people more concerned. Sometimes that isn't a bad thing.

10 FEBRUARY 2012

Abu Saber (@Moawen)
In the last Friday before #feb14 , tens of thousands of protesters marched to freedom square in #Bahrain http://pic.twitter.com/N6YwY3TP

Albahraini (@alhojairy)
Now thousands protesters chanting "down with hamad" referring to the king of #bahrain

Self-determination (@Takrooz)
It is 3 days, 9 hours, 12 minutes, 6 seconds until Tuesday, February 14, 2012

Last night I went with a Bahraini friend and my son to the Bahrain International Circuit to see the drag races. Rather than take the highway, we took the direct route, which passes through all the villages. In the village of Hamala, for about a hundred yards the road was covered with bricks, cinderblocks, trees, and other debris. We had to zigzag our way through it all. My friend assured me that Sunnis and Shi'a here don't have any problem with each other, and it was just the government that was making things hard. I think that was mostly true before last year, but now I believe Sunnis are getting increasingly frustrated with the inconveniences created by the constant, low-level demonstrations, and their impact on the economy.

Today, I went with a friend to visit a family in our church. On our way we passed over the Burgerland Roundabout (pictured above) as thousands of people marched to Freedom Square, an open area further down on Budaiyah Highway. It caused a little traffic as they blocked off the exits, and people watched from the overpass.

People are saying that on the twelfth they will to march from the area villages to try to retake the Pearl Roundabout. I'm guessing the twelfth will be a halfhearted attempt of probably around 10,000 people. On the fourteenth, I predict over 30,000 people will march. Ten or twenty thousand people will get close enough to be affected by the tear gas. Five to ten thousand will get close enough to get hit with rubber bullets. One to five thousand will get close enough to try to breach the barbed wire and risk getting hit with batons. They will do everything they can to appear as peaceful as possible, because they know the eyes of the world will be on them. They will leave the Molotov cocktails at home. I expect five to ten people will die, and hundreds will be hospitalized.

12 FEBRUARY 2012

Abu-sajad (@kingofmaxima)
most of #Bahrain's roads are blocked by security forces & national guard in trying to prevent people to go to martyrs square.

AquaMarine (@Aquamarine155)
"In the End, we will remember not the words of our enemies, but the silence of our friends." - Martin Luther King Jr. #bahrain #freedom

Yesterday afternoon, my wife was driving with a friend past the Grand Mosque (which is Sunni). She saw a large crowd walking towards the mosque. They appeared to be cheering and thanking the police. Many cars driving by had people—including children—hanging half out of the car, waving Bahraini flags and smiling. She said all the cars seemed to be expensive, luxury cars, and the display presented quite a contrast to the Shi'a demonstrators. The perception is the Sunni want to show their support for the government and make sure that their voices are heard by all the relevant parties.

Today, I drove around the area between the Souk and the Seef District, which includes the former Pearl Roundabout. The police had set up checkpoints on roads leading into this area. There were now men in uniform, likely the Bahraini National Guard, posted at different points. They had two rows of razor wire surrounding the approximately two-thirds of a kilometer formerly known as the Pearl Roundabout, but which has since been renamed Farouq Junction by the government.

Two days ago the police were mostly sitting back, and some were even smoking. Now they were standing alert, with rifles in their arms. I don't know what type of rounds the guns were loaded with, but probably rubber bullets, and the soldiers were likely equipped with tear gas and rubber batons as well. They had armored vehicles with manned gun turrets with National Guard written in Arabic on the license plates.

Roads leading towards Budaiyah Highway in the direction of the Burgerland Roundabout were also blocked. Traffic was bad, and people were expecting things to start happening. They even canceled my son's practice tonight because of the uncertainty about what would happen. I suspect a lot of things will be canceled over the next couple of days. I've heard media reports about different attempts to approach the Pearl Roundabout. There will likely be others tomorrow. I expect most people are "keeping their powder dry," so to speak, saving it for the fourteenth.

14 FEBRUARY 2012

Dr. Wafa Alnoaimi (@Aljazita)
MANY BAHRAINI CITIZENS ARE NOW BEING ARRESTED ALL OVER #BAHRAIN INSTEAD OF RELEASING POLITICAL PRISONERS THEY R JAILING MORE #witnessbahrain

BahrainOnline (@ONLINEBAHRAIN)
Freedom fighters vacated their cars near Dana Mall and ran towards #Lulu but were attacked brutally #Bahrain #Feb14 #LuluReturn

Abu Ali (@RARAR_14F)
#14Feb #USA #UK This what the (#Bahrain) worst regime did today for peaceful people. http://yfrog.com/kec1mfbj

Abdul Hamid Ahmad (@AbdulHamidAhmad)
King Hamad highlights cohesion as way forward for Bahrain: http://bit.ly/xwPMSM

ش———ح———و‎‎اال ل (@sha7oooooal)
We must stand together in defense of our bahrain and our laws against
the advocates of sedition and evil poles at home and abroad #world #ff

Today was the anniversary of the uprising. We all waited anxious-
ly for 3:00 p.m., when the protests were scheduled to begin. I came
across a website that showed the live traffic camera video feeds of the
key areas where the demonstrators would likely advance to the Pearl
Roundabout. Not long after 4:00 p.m., they put out a message saying
the live feed was no longer active. No doubt the government wanted
to control the flow of information. There were numerous reports of
several groups getting turned away by the police and National Guard
as they approached the Pearl, as well as reports of many people getting
wounded and arrested. The police successfully kept the crowds divided, and the protestors were therefore unable to form a critical mass
that could approach the area all at one time. Armored vehicles were a
common sight in many areas around town.

My wife hosted a Valentine's Day Party this afternoon from 4 to
6 p.m. for families in our housing compound. After it was over and
the children were playing outside one of the workers told everyone to
go inside because a little tear gas was blowing over the walls. Likely,
it was coming from a neighboring Shi'a village. The children all explained to me what tear gas feels like.

I had to work late, and when I drove home around 7:30 p.m. through
the Pearl Roundabout and Budaiyah Highway area, there weren't a lot
of cars on the road, and those that were either raced by really fast or
drove really slowly. The security forces were still out, but the people
had left the area. In some areas, you could smell smoke, and near my
house, there were obstructions in the road.

No doubt we'll hear more tomorrow about everything that happened tonight. Likely many battles will continue, and it seems the
police have increased the use of rubber bullets. The protestors say
they will try again over the next few days to march towards the Pearl
Roundabout, but I think if they couldn't do it today, they're going to
have to come up with some other plan. This will likely frustrate those
who wanted to achieve their aims through traditional protest activity. I
expect we will now see more people willing to be more aggressive in

their confrontations with the police. They will consider new ways to cause disruption to the life here to increase the pressure on the government to agree to their goals.

19 FEBRUARY 2012

jaffer alaali (@jaffer_alaali)

Expats leading an unauthorized protest in Bahrain http://fb.me/NDf83F6x

#LuluReturn @Amh_Dz believe me i know many of those stories,so much that am drowning in them!..wounded still in jail,nearly die,bad shape! YES its #Bahrain

Even though the tens of thousands didn't march to the Pearl Roundabout on the fourteenth as expected, over the past five days small groups, most in the ten- to forty-year-old age range, attempted to reach the area many are calling LuLu Square as Lulu is the Arabic word for pearl. The government has introduced a new crowd control method—the hot water cannons. It is hard for me to imagine how they can keep the temperature of the water within the small range uncomfortable enough to affect an angry protester, without causing burns.

Several Americans have been arrested and deported for marching with the protesters. They came here on tourist visas and were deported for lying about the intended purpose of their visit.

The confrontations continue every day in areas like Sitra, villages near the Pearl Roundabout like Sanabis, Al-Daih, and Jidh Hafs, and the villages along Budaiyah Highway. I hear reports of how businesses are really struggling to survive in these areas. The economic impact will take a toll, both on the government and on the Shi'a in these areas.

I read an article about the use of pipe bombs against the police. I suppose this isn't a surprising evolution when revolutionary groups begin to see the futility of traditional protest methods. I expect over the coming months to see new violent tactics, slowly increasing in sophistication. More moderate elements of the opposition will look for other ways to keep the pressure on the government.

21 FEBRUARY 2012

Andrew Hammond (@Hammonda1)
Heavy anti-Iran/US rhetoric from Salafi sheikhs at Fateh rally, incl Abdullah al-Nifeesy warning 'the new Qarmatians' r coming #bahrain

Sahwat Al-Fatih EN (@Sahwat_AlFatih)
We demand the activation of the Gulf confederation to stand up against Iran and the lies which it has been spreading #Bahrain #21feb

rosamund de sybel (@rosdesybel)
Al Fateh march looks as if its going to be huge, lots of families on foot (!!) walking from Adliya #Bahrain

On my way home from work I drove past the Al-Fateh (Grand) Mosque about an hour before a planned rally intended to show support for the government. The atmosphere seemed like that at a major sports event. A lot of people were walking on the sidewalks and crossing the streets. About one in five cars had a Bahraini flag attached or waving out the window. People were honking horns, and one car full of women had a couple of them standing up through the sunroof, waving flags. Many of the people walking towards the mosque were carrying flags, and a few had them draped around their shoulders like capes. The only police there were traffic police, who naturally were directing traffic.

One estimate put the attendance at between twenty and thirty thousand people. The statements at the rally served to discourage compromise, but also attempted to show that there were other constituencies in Bahrain that needed to be heard.

26 FEBRUARY 2012

Ministry of Interior (@moi_bahrain)
Interior Minister: We overcame hindrances, brought about unity &stop abusers thanks to our trust in the leadership #Bahrain

matthew cassel (@justimage)
Bahrain human rights activist Abdulhadi al-Khawaja is on day 16 without eating to protest his detention. Follow hashtag: #hungry4BH

There is still no clear indication of which way the unrest is going to go after 14 February, but things have eased up a bit. The street battles with police seem to have lost a little of their intensity, but I suspect it is just a lull in the cycle, waiting for the next flashpoint. Yesterday, there was a coordinated attempt to burn tires and block traffic. While watching my son's game at a field near Riffa, I could see a column of black smoke rising a few blocks away.

It is fascinating to see what tactics the protestors will come up with next. A prominent activist is on his sixteenth day of a hunger strike. His death would bring major media attention and definitely stir things up again.

8 MARCH 2012

GCC Citizen (@Life4BH)
Congrats to all who got jobs back after paid 1 year leave including bonuses & extra allowances Wish I called 4 death of king like u #Bahrain

Lamees Dhaif (@LameesDhaif)
Persians defeated Portuguese & ruled #Bahrain from 1521-1700 AD. Therefore some Persians outdate Al Khalifa in their existence on this land

fred willie (@fredwillie460)
#Bahrain democracy under attack - Shia clerics issue Fatwas to compel their flocks to attend mass anti-everybody else rally tomorrow

Shehab Hashem (@hashem911)
Don't race in #Bahrain - F1 shame on you. Protest outside the #F1 Management building now.

A police car was burned in Al-Dair, and four policemen were seriously injured. Sheikh Isa Qassim has called for all his supporters to march from Saar to the Meqsha/Country Mall area, over three kilometers away, tomorrow at 3:00 p.m. There will likely be tens of thousands involved, as he is the most prominent Shi'a cleric in Bahrain. It seems people are trying to figure out where things go from here, and he naturally stepped in to provide some leadership. He hasn't publicly called for a gathering since last year. Sunnis decided to organize a counter-rally in support of the government to be held at the same time in Muharraq.

It has occurred to me that nearly all of the posts on social media sites are designed to rally a particular side and usually seem to alienate the others. Social media has played a key role in facilitating protest activity in other countries. I can see now how it fosters sectarian conflict.

Groups have called for the Formula One organizers to reverse their decision to hold the event here in Bahrain. Some have even promised to try to disrupt the event. Similar to what was going on during the Bahrain International Airshow, there will likely be roadblocks and fires across the country, and perhaps even more aggressive attempts to prevent the event from going smoothly.

12 MARCH 2012

angry arabiya (@angryarabiya)
Bani Jamra under attack now, more than 20 riot police jeeps. The cowards come in huge numbers for the brave revolutionaries #Bahrain

Saeed Shehabi (@SaeedShehabi)
Bahrain's rally was the biggest in the world in terms of participants to population ratio. If this is not a revolution, what is? #Bahrain

Ministry of Interior (@moi_bahrain)
After a burial in Deraz, rioters blocked roads & committed acts of vandalism. Police restored order #Bahrain

The protest march a couple days ago had between 100,000 and 200,000 people. A couple hours before the scheduled 3:00 p.m. start time, cars were backed up for about a kilometer trying to get into the area. There are roughly 600,000 Bahraini citizens, of whom 400,000 are Shi'a, so minus the children, senior citizens, and people who had to work, the number of protestors at that march represents a very high proportion of the population. Sheikh Isa Qassim and other moderate Shi'a leaders wanted to show broad support for their demands. I think they accomplished that.

I heard that the signs held by the marchers ranged from rejectionist calls such as "Down, Down Hamad" to more conciliatory calls for democracy. As they neared the later half of the march, the women went down one side of the two-lane road, and the men went down the other. There were small groups (probably less than a hundred each) skirmishing with security forces, but these were much milder than during the marches last month. Driving around, I noticed the burned remnants of roadblocks on major roads in several areas.

24 MARCH 2012

benwedeman (@bencnn)
Interesting to hear Al-Manar (Hizballah TV) newsreader in one breath condemning #Syria uprising and supporting #Bahrain opposition.

Emile Hokayem (@emile_hokayem)
Bahrain RT @glcarlstrom Sitra looks like war zone, smashed windows, roads littered w/bricks, stones, stench of tear gas+smoke

Ministry of Interior (@moi_bahrain)
Vedio shows rioting and vandalism by a group of the participants of Al Wefaq rallies #Bahrain
http://www.youtube.com/watch?v=se5PSqwkI2c

Abu Saber (@Moawen)
Thousands of angry protesters in Tubli #Bahrain demanding to overthrow the regime http://www.youtube.com/watch?v=_bYILN-J1ErM #Bahrain10Marches

Two days ago, five Shi'a political societies (including the largest, Al-Wefaq) jointly organized rallies across Bahrain...mainly in the traditional areas: Saar/Budaiyah Highway, south of the Pearl Roundabout (Sanabis/Jidh Hafs/Bilad al-Qadeem), Tubli, Sitra, and others. The majority of the demonstrations were peaceful, but there were skirmishes with police. There was also a Sunni rally in Hidd, mainly to show they were against further negotiation and concessions.

The routine continues: a road is blocked; police come to clear it; youth battle with the police; and then tear gas is used to disperse. Periodically, I see images of police vehicles being burned and read occasional press reports of policemen injured and some hospitalized. However, there is a perception that things are not going to get worse and that things will continue as they are for a long time to come. The worry that everyone had before the 14 February anniversary has subsided.

A few days ago, my wife and a friend who works at Salmaniya Hospital arranged to bring gifts and toys to children in the hospital. Although I wasn't here last year, I read press reports of the government believing that the hospital had been taken over by the demonstrators. As we entered the parking lot, there was a normal police checkpoint with several armed men sitting on chairs. They looked at me closely but didn't indicate for me to stop. As my family walked through the halls, there were unarmed security guards at almost every junction. We stopped for a picture in a quiet hallway. Quickly, a security guard stopped us and told us there was no photography allowed.

Today, when my son was in the middle of a sports match, a thick column of black smoke started billowing on the other side of the wall. It appeared to be relatively close to the wall, about fifty meters away. I asked the coach if he minded if I walked back there to have a look, and he said that was fine with him. I wanted to see what was burning and if there was any other activity associated with it. The wall was probably around nine feet high, with wrought iron bars sticking out of the top. I jumped up and pulled myself up by the bars. There wasn't a single person around. A barricade of tires and wooden debris was burning across the road. I wondered whether the location was chosen specifically so we would see it and be witnesses to their frustration. Within a few minutes, we heard sirens and a few minutes after that the fire was out.

I asked one of my Bahraini friends, Mohammed, to give me a report of the things he was witnessing. These next three entries—April 1, 2 and 5—are from him, as are several other entries in April and May.

1 APRIL 2012 (MOHAMMED)

Ahmad Esmail, an eighteen-year old Shi'a from Salmabad, was killed during demonstrations. The young Shi'a was shot in the stomach and was transported to a hospital, where he was pronounced dead. Several demonstrations took place as a result. The most confrontational protest took place on Saturday, 31 March 2012, in the village of Al-Dair. Shi'a attacked anti-riot police, causing severe injuries to one local policeman. In Sanabis, another demonstration took place where Shi'a burned tires and blocked roads. Nabeel Rajab, a human rights activist, was arrested on Friday, 30 March after he participated in an unauthorized protest in Manama. In Sitra, Shi'a blocked the main Sitra causeway to protest the killing of Ahmad Esmail. On Friday night, Sunnis in Bahrain organized a large festival in support of Syria. Sunnis raised money for the people of Syria during the event. During the event the crowd chanted anti-Bashar al-Assad slogans.

Some Shi'a in area villages are speculating that the shooting of Ahmad Esmail may be retaliation for the Omar feet-kissing incident. Omar is a young boy—five years old—whose teacher told him to kiss her feet every morning. The teacher is a Shi'a woman who teaches at Al Noor International School. Sunnis were furious when they heard about the incident last week. The incident was covered by a dozen satellite televisions from Lebanon to Egypt. On Friday, 30 March, Sunni sermons were dominated by this Omar story. Omar is a very important and sensitive name for the Sunnis, as they admire Caliph Omar, who took over from Caliph Abu Bakr al-Sadiq. Sunnis view the teacher forcing Omar to kiss her feet as a sectarian action, an insult from a Shi'a woman to a Sunni caliph known to be hated by Shi'a. Some Sunni extremists went as far as putting the woman on a death list. They sent her and her husband life-threatening messages, which causes her to stay home.

2 APRIL 2012 (MOHAMMED)

Shi'a protestors burned two police vehicles on A'ali Highway, just about three kilometers from Seef Mall Highway. Shi'a claim that the attack on the two vehicles is part of a series of planned attacks to protest the Grand Prix event, scheduled to take place in Bahrain at the end of April 2012. The two vehicles were seen blazing along the highway while the local police awaited assistance. Rumors are going around about unknown civilians wearing ski masks, randomly shooting into the air while patrolling in Diraz. Shi'a responded by throwing rocks. No one was hurt during the incident. There is no confirmation whether live ammunition was used, but Shi'a circulated pictures of the bullets.

5 APRIL 2012 (MOHAMMED)

Intense fighting between police and protesters took place in Sanabis on 5 April, in the afternoon. The confrontation began when protesters were organizing a demonstration in support of Abdulhadi Alkhawaja, a human rights activist who is detained. Alkhawaja went on hunger strike about a month ago. Several armored vehicles were attacked with Molotov cocktails. Tear gas was widely used to disperse the crowd.

In Karbabad, Shi'a burned tires in close proximity to Seef Mall, causing a major traffic jam. Anti-riot police responded with tear gas.

While being chased by Shi'a protestors, a police vehicle lost control and turned over in the village of Sitra. All five members of the police who had been in the car were transported to BDF hospital. Some injuries were serious.

From social media, it looks like Shi'a opposition groups plan to escalate their violent activity in the coming days because of the F1 event, and because Alkhawaja's health is deteriorating as a result of his hunger strike. A health expert said that Alkhawaja might not make it if he continues on the hunger strike.

6 APRIL 2012

Gregg Carlstrom (@glcarlstrom)
Police have not made a single arrest after 54 attacks on Jawad stores during the past year: http://bit.ly/HkNimp #bahrain

Rasha Abdulla (@RashaAbdulla)
Doctors say human rights activist Abdulhadi #Alkhawaja is at severe risk of eminent organ failure on day 57 of hunger strike. #Bahrain

bahraini mother (@Sabeeda_trend)
Everyone is talking about saving #alkawja he starved himself let him die the way he want #bahrain

Earlier this week in a cabinet meeting, Prime Minister Khalifa bin Salman al-Khalifa announced a plan to build three thousand new homes and urged authorities to step up work on housing, municipal, road-network and infrastructure projects directly linked to citizens' daily lives. This seems to be an attempt to address some of the peripheral grievances and ease tension without having to make serious reforms.

The Jawad chain of grocery stores is owned by a prominent Shi'a family in Bahrain. Jawad and other Shi'a stores have been attacked, presumably by Sunnis frustrated with the unrest. There have also been reports of Sunnis boycotting Shi'a businesses. It is the sectarian tension that is more likely to bring widespread violence here than anything else.

Later on tonight, a little after five, I went with my children to visit someone from my church. We exited at the Burgerland Roundabout and headed towards Manama, passing through Jidh Hafs. As we approached the roundabout, we could see smoke rising in the distance, about a kilometer ahead. As we drove past the International Hospital of Bahrain, I could see the smoke was coming from the next round about. As I approached the roundabout, I saw that a few cars were going around it in the wrong direction, and I soon saw that on the opposite side, the road entering the roundabout was blocked with burning tires. Other cars cautiously went other directions or up onto the curb. One car finally burst right through the burning barricade.

As we continued on our way, we saw a lot of people walking the opposite direction to the way we were going. Several of them had "Free Khawaja" posters. One lady dressed in all black wore a red headband with a slogan that started with the words, "We Sacrifice," but I couldn't read the rest. I was surprised to see Nabeel Rajab, who I recognized from the news and social media sites, casually walking by. The road opened up to a wider gathering area where there were approximately five hundred people milling around. It seemed as though the demonstration had already ended, but I wasn't sure.

Suddenly, some of the people started moving quickly, and the cars stopped. A tear gas canister landed in the road two or three cars ahead of me. Three or four more landed in the same area, and suddenly there was a thick wall of tear gas. There was a metal fence to my left and no road on the right. We were trapped.

I turned off the air conditioning and told the children to hold their breath. I slowly drove about fifteen yards through the noxious cloud, not able to see anything in front of me. When I came out the other side, I saw a young man calmly but briskly walking past me with an unlit Molotov cocktail. A few anti-riot policemen emerged onto the street from left. Crowds were running in the opposite direction. Barricades seemed to appear out of nowhere, and there wasn't anywhere for me to turn around. One guy who was running past motioned for me to turn around. Some of the roads were blocked with boards with many nails sticking out as spikes; others were blocked with cinderblocks.

I could see the water cannon trucks about four hundred yards down the road, but moving steadily towards us, blasting people along the way. I finally found an unblocked road, which I creatively made my way through by driving down the wrong lane. I slowly made my way through the narrow village streets, trying to quickly circle back to head down the road I had come down. People were moving quickly down every narrow street. When I came to the street that I had hoped would connect with the main road, it appeared that it didn't, and about fifteen people were standing there, blocking the way. I gestured as if to ask if there was a way through. One man said no, but then realized where I needed to go and moved the people out of the way.

I was soon back on the main road, about forty meters in front of the water cannons. I slowed down to drive through a small pile of bricks on the road, and then drove halfway up the high curb to get past a cinder block barricade. There weren't any other cars around.

I soon learned why. As I drove forward, I suddenly saw that the road was completely blocked with dumpsters, wood, and other debris. There was a group of people on the other side, presumably waiting to confront the police. The water cannon trucks and other police vehicles were closing in behind me. The metal railing prevented me from crossing over to the other lane, and the side roads to my right led into the Shi'a neighborhood, which might not have been a good place for me to go. Even if it had been, it didn't matter. All those side roads were blocked, so that wasn't even an option. Once again, we were trapped.

I drove quickly in reverse about fifty meters to see if there was a break in the metal railing where I could cross over. There wasn't. I finally saw an opening among the houses, a street leading back into the neighborhood I had just emerged from. I saw a couple of cars that looked like they knew where they were going, and I followed them. We finally went down a small hill and across a large dirt field. People were still running around, and it seemed on every street people were looking out the windows or standing in the doorways.

I came out the other side of Sanabis, near the Bahrain Mall, and we continued on our way. We happened to go past the former Pearl Roundabout, and the police and National Guard stationed there seemed more alert than usual. My children didn't seem any more concerned than I was, and we talked about how we never see this type of thing, but that it nevertheless goes on regularly.

It is amazing how Westerners living away from the Shi'a villages can on with their regular lives here and yet not see very much of the unrest that happens everyday. I regularly hear visitors express their surprise at how normal things are. Even some of those who live here aren't aware that every night there are violent confrontations between protestors and the police. I would estimate that activity on the scale of what the children and I had just experienced happens every few days, or at the least, every week or so.

13 APRIL 2012 (MOHAMMED)

Moosa Abd Ali collapsed after nine days on hunger strike outside the US Embassy in London and was taken to the hospital Friday, 13 April 2012. Ali Mushayma, the son of Hassan Mushayma, is still on a hunger strike across from the US Embassy in London. He refused to leave the area or to eat, even after local officials insisted he do so.

The Bahrain Al-Ahli bank was vandalized and burned by Shi'a in Sanabis on 1 April 2012 in an attempt to escalate Shi'a activity against the government before the final decision about whether to proceed with the Formula 1 race. That decision is scheduled to be announced today, 13 April.

A homemade bomb exploded on Exhibition Road, damaging three cars but no injuries were reported. A Shi'a splinter group claimed responsibility and promised more attacks if the F1 event goes ahead as scheduled. Another IED that targeted security forces in Bahrain exploded in Eker on 09 April 2012. A different splinter group claimed responsibility for this incident.

Shi'a in Al-Dair burned a dozen tires just a few meters from the back fence of Bahrain International Airport. Smoke could be seen from a few kilometers away, as Shi'a violence begins to take a different spin before the F1 announcement. In Bani Jamra, there was intense fighting between Shi'a and security forces. Tear gas was used to disperse the crowd.

A group of Sunnis vandalized a Jawad store on 10 April in Riffa after a demonstration against Shi'a. Sunnis were protesting against the Eker explosion. Confrontations between the police and Sunnis took place as the police tried to stop Sunnis from marching into Shi'a villages to retaliate for the Eker incident.

15 APRIL 2012

Ahmed Al Awadhi (@Ah_Alawadhi)
I don't know what the key to success is, but the key to failure is trying to please everyone. #BAHRAIN #PPL #FACT

Asad bahrain (@asadbahrain)
Bahrain Youth rebel burning car & tires in main highway(threat to #F1) http://fb.me/1FEJ0VvS2 #GP @f1_vettel @f1_webber @Formula1_com

I drove home late tonight from work, around 8:15, and for about thirty minutes, I was stuck in slow-moving traffic on the highway leading to the Saudi Causeway. I finally came upon the remnants of a burning roadblock not far from Al-Wefaq headquarters. It was still smoking, and a fire truck off the side of the road was responding to it.

A bomb went off in the Hoora/Exhibition Road area a couple days ago that some people were saying was a propane tank, and others were saying was a pipe bomb. This is not a traditional protest area and is where a lot of tourists come to socialize. The upcoming Formula 1 race will likely bring the unrest out of the traditional areas. Police seem to be reacting more aggressively, and there have been a few reports about them now using shotguns, or bird shot. This is likely a result of the Eker bombing and trying to be more firm leading up to the race.

I saw a post on a social media site about another incident of a Sunni attack on a Shi'a store in Busaiteen. A few clerics have made an effort to calm the sectarian tension, but I think the factions are nearing the point where a deal will be impossible to reach and the downward spiral of sectarian strife will continue.

19 APRIL 2012

As I was exiting the highway in the evening from the Seef Area onto the Burgerland Roundabout, cars about a hundred meters ahead me suddenly came to a stop. As I slowed down, I saw a group of young men carrying things onto the road, and then I saw a Molotov cocktail fly onto the road. They appeared to be trying to ignite the trees they had laid across the road. A few cars quickly reversed past me, but I decided to wait. Police ran over to respond, and a policeman standing right behind my car fired several rounds of tear gas at the group of about six young men, who by then were running away across a sandy field. After a few minutes, the police had pushed the burning debris far enough to the side to let us pass.

28 APRIL 2012

Bahrain_moi (@Ministry of Interior)
A shooting took place at a building in the Central Governorate today morning. The police launched investigation #Bahrain

The Formula 1 race proceeded without any major disruptions. There were a lot of tire burnings and intense demonstration activity in the days surrounding the race, but nothing that prevented people from attending. The government probably succeeded in using the international event to maintain the perception that Bahrain is a safe place to visit and do business in, although it did bring renewed media scrutiny of the situation here.

There have been a couple more instances of improvised explosive devices being used against police, severely injuring some police officers. This attempt to increase pressure on the government to make concessions runs the risk of increasing the divide between the two communities and making it easier for the government to portray the opposition as violent extremists. Although these attacks don't represent the entire Shi'a opposition, the government will likely try to paint it that way. A couple of fake IEDs have been left in some areas to send a message about what the protestors are capable of doing. One was even left outside a business in Juffair where the US Navy has its headquarters, likely an attempt to send a message to the US government.

It is hard to see where this ends. Violent exchanges occur almost nightly. The Shi'a commitment to achieving their goals shows no sign of letting up, and the government seems willing to make only modest reforms that fall far short of what is demanded by the opposition. Perhaps it will continue on this general path until the prime minister, who is reportedly around eighty years old, passes away. I think only then will the king be willing to have a prime minister selected by representatives of the people. It can't be easy to fire your uncle and his large staff, especially since that too includes extended family.

30 APRIL 2012 (MOHAMMED)

On 29 April 2012, Shi'a in Al-Dair burned a large number of tires in the vicinity of Bahrain International Airport. The smoke was so thick it could be seen from Amwaj Island. Anti-riot police arrived at the scene and immediately used tear gas to disperse a large Shi'a crowd gathered at the entrance of Al-Dair.

On 28 April Shi'a blocked the main entrance to Sitra, causing a major traffic jam. When anti-riot police arrived, Shi'a attacked with Molotov cocktails. A Sunni parliamentarian named Al-Tameemi accused followers of the prime minister of throwing Molotov cocktails on his compound in Sanad. A few days ago, Al-Tameemi urged the prime minister to resign and accused him of delaying reforms in Bahrain.

On 26 April Shi'a in Karbabad blocked the major roads leading to Seef Mall with tires, causing a major traffic jam. The police arrived on the scene and a confrontation between the police and Shi'a took place. Anti-riot police used tear gas, forcing the Shi'a to retreat.

On Tuesday, 24 April a homemade bomb rocked the village of Diraz, causing injuries to a number of anti-riot police. According to witnesses, Shi'a lured anti-riot police to the area of the bomb by claiming there was a fire in the area. When anti-riot police arrived at the scene accompanying the firefighters, the explosion took place. A Shi'a opposition group claimed responsibility.

Sunnis are pressuring the government to protect Ministry of Interior security forces by supplying them with firearms to defend themselves. Sunnis blame the government of Bahrain for abandoning its people, who are responsible for defending the island and the regime. Shi'a are planning to take advantage of the Labor Day holiday on May 1 to hold a number of demonstrations throughout Bahrain.

Shi'a hard-line groups in Bahrain have increased their violent activity after the grand prix event. According to witnesses, at least a dozen vehicles were burned in various areas, including Diraz, Sitra, Sanabis, Al-Dair, and Damustan.

9 MAY 2012 (MOHAMMED)

In Bani Jamra on 6 May, the local police found an IED device that did not go off. Also on 6 May, in Al-Dair, Shi'a completely burned and destroyed a police vehicle after luring it deep inside the village.

On 7 May, Shi'a burned tires in Sitra in an attempt to block the main highway and the entrance to the village. When the police arrived, Shi'a demonstrators threw Molotov cocktails and fled the area.

Sunnis praised comments by Prime Minister Al Khalifa about political comments during religious sermons. The prime minister recommended more restrictions on the content of Friday sermons. Sunnis believe that the new rule may be targeted against Isa Qassim.

According to witnesses, the government has begun using robots to detonate explosives in an attempt to protect its security forces. The new equipment has been used in Sitra and Diraz in the past few days as the police discovered fake bombs.

Shi'a youth continue to target Batelco call centers in area villages. The cost of each center is between fifteen and twenty thousand US dollars. Shi'a have been burning these centers in A'ali, Salmabad, Hamad Town, and Sitra. Shi'a are targeting Batelco because it is partly owned by the prime minister.

11 MAY 2012

Ministry of Interior (@moi_bahrain)
Groups of thugs blocked various roads today morning. Legal proce-
dures were taken and the situation was brought to normal

WikiLeaks (@wikileaks)
Nabeel Rajab detained on 5/5 heads to trial with 13 others on 22/5 in
Bahrain. That date? Day before the Egyptian election wipes the news.

AlwefaqEN (@AlWefaqEN)
A stand in solidrraty with sh.Qassim rejecting late offenses by the
press against sh.Qassim

Nabeel Rajab was arrested on 05 May 2012, when he stepped
off the plane in Bahrain. He was returning from a trip he had taken
to interview Julian Assange of Wikileaks. The government arrested
him for his tweets encouraging protest activity, for leading "unauthorized" demonstrations and criticizing the government. This has brought
widespread criticism from human rights groups and has infuriated the
Shi'a opposition. This led to rumors and speculation that leaders such
as Sheikh Isa Qassim might be arrested or banned from giving public
sermons. The prime minister fed this speculation a couple days ago by
warning leaders about crossing the line of appropriate public speech.

Isa Qassim made a speech a few months ago in which he said that
if you see the police harming a woman, you should "Crush them!"
Many Sunnis blame this speech for causing the increase in violence.
Today, thousands of Shi'a rallied outside the mosque in Diraz that Isa
Qassim attends to show their support. I think banning his speeches will
only make people more interested in what he is saying and inflame the
situation even more.

Yesterday there was a coordinated effort to block many of the
major roads during the morning commute. My usual twenty-five min-
ute commute turned into an hour and fifteen minutes. The police are
usually very fast at removing roadblocks. However, there have been
several instances of explosive devices being placed in the burning debris, which have been detonated just as the police came to remove it.

Naturally the police are more reluctant to move the roadblocks and now wait for bomb technicians to check for possible devices. Sometimes hoax devices are placed to cause police to hesitate before they get near it. There have also been a couple of hoax bombs left in the area near the American Navy Base.

16 MAY 2012

Ministry of Interior (@moi_bahrain)
A group of thugs hindered traffic on Shaikh Khalifa bin Salman RD towards the west. Police at the scene to bring traffic flow to normal

Ministry of Interior (@moi_bahrain)
The search had been intensified to arrest the suspects to execute the orders obtained from Pub Prosecutor #BAH

Quite Bahrain-i (@QuiteBH)
can they at least declare #Bahrain a natural reservation and stop the #shotgun hunting of protesters!!

Yesterday, Shi'a 14 February Coalition groups conducted another coordinated campaign to block roads across the island during the morning commute. This one wasn't quite as effective and seemed to occur mostly in Shi'a neighborhoods, with a few other attempts to the block the road on some major highways. There were several videos posted, usually showing a group of ten to fifteen masked young men running into the street carrying tires, pouring gas or oil on the tires, and then setting them on fire. Again they placed hoax bombs near some of the roadblocks to delay their removal. On the front page of the *Gulf Daily News* today were the names and faces of twenty individuals wanted for bombings that have hospitalized several policemen.

Tomorrow there is supposed to be a massive demonstration on Budaiyah Highway heading towards Diraz to protest the proposed Bahrain-Saudi unity plan, the approval of US weapon sales to Bahrain, and other issues. My neighbor told me his company told him to stay inside all weekend if possible. He is new to Bahrain and told me about the panic he experienced seeing the burning tires and tear gas fired in Adliya, and seeing the cars turn around and drive back the wrong way down the road.

Some of the main political societies released a letter today about the alleged abuse of Shi'a prisoners:

In a letter from the prisoners to the people of Bahrain, they described the many violations committed by the police inside detention camp number 9. The letter says they have faced sexual harassment, brutal beatings, verbal abuse and religious discrimination. In addition, their regular visits have been deliberately delayed and they have been denied necessary medical treatment.

We, the opposition parties, express our deep concern regarding the awful conditions in Dry Dock detention camp, which violates the basic human rights of prisoners, guaranteed by the international treaties signed by the Bahrain government.

These claims from the prisoners warrant an immediate inspection visit that must be conducted by local and international human rights organisations. This inspection should look into all allegations of mistreatment and should involve direct interviews with the prisoners.

An investigation should also take place to address the discrimination of beliefs and religion faced by the prisoners. The prison administration personnel who commit such violations must be brought to justice to guarantee that this dangerous situation is stopped.

The violations taking place in Dry Dock Prison make clear to the international community the systematic and repressive security strategy practiced by this government. This government has no respect to either the findings of the Bahrain Independent Commission of Inquiry; in terms of implementing it's recommendations, nor the international human rights treaties.

Long live a free and democratic Bahrain.

- Al-Wefaq National Islamic Society
- National Democratic Action Society (Waad)
- Nationalist Democratic Assembly Society
- Alekha National Society
- National Democratic Assemblage (Unitary)

20 MAY 2012 (MOHAMMED)

A large demonstration took place on the afternoon of Friday, 18 May in support of Isa Qassim, and to show strong opposition to the purported union of Bahrain and Saudi Arabia. Thousands of Shi'a attended the event, which took place from Shakhura to Diraz Roundabout. While supporters of Al-Wefaq chanted slogans in support of Qassim, the followers of the 14 February Coalition (the groups that call for an end to King Hamad's rule) chanted "The people still want to overthrow the regime."

It felt like there were two demonstrations, two crowds, two messages, two different directions. The difference between Al-Wefaq and the 14 February Coalition was very clear and was demonstrated in many ways. While supporters of Al-Wefaq held pictures of Qassim, supporters of the Shi'a 14 February Coalition displayed pictures of Abdulwahab Hussein, Mushayma, Al-Maqdad, Nabeel Rajab, Al-Khawaja, and other Shi'a clerics and activists. While Al-Wefaq insisted on chanting against the proposed Saudi-Bahrain union, the 14 February Coalition insisted on overthrowing the regime. While Al-Wefaq refrained from any anti-US chanting, the 14 February Coalition consistently chanted anti-US slogans during the event. A small crowd burned US flags in Diraz after the event ended.

On Saturday, 19 May 2012, Sunnis tried to respond to the large Shi'a event by organizing a gathering next to Al-Fateh Mosque in a show of support to the union. The event was a failure from the beginning, as not all Sunnis were in favor of the event. The Sunni Salafis were completely against it, as they feared that the media might focus on the relative sizes of the crowd to determine that a larger portion of the population (Shi'a) was against the union. The organizers did not get the support they sought from Sunni clerics, who usually urge people during Friday sermon to attend such events. Overall the crowd was large, but not as large as that attending the Shi'a event. This event was also affected by the deep religious and political divisions within Sunni groups.

Violence continued in area villages this weekend. In Al-Dair on Friday, 18 May, there was a violent confrontation between Shi'a and anti-riot police, during a demonstration called "Let them burn in hell."

This demonstration was against the US and the Al Khalifa regime, both of which Shi'a blame for the proposed union between Saudi Arabia and Bahrain.

In Sitra, fighting was intense between Shi'a and security forces. On Saturday, 19 May, Shi'a burned tires and blocked the Sitra Causeway, causing a major traffic jam. Shi'a also ambushed security forces during their routine patrols in and around the villages. Shi'a staged a massive attack using Molotov cocktails and firework launchers against the local police station.

22 MAY 2012

Myrtha (@juhui67)
SHAME on you Queen! #DiamondJubilee :(((RT"@EleiaAli: The Butcher of #Bahrain has no place at Buckingham Palace

BahrainOnline (@ONLINEBAHRAIN)
Tens of Thousands Protest in Bahrain Against 'Saudi Union' http://ow.ly/b0YQv #Bahrain #Saudi

Abdulla Bin Nabeel (@Abdulla_Nabeel)
A #civilian car was burned due to proiranian thughs in #Bahrain

There were rallies in Iran about the proposed Saudi-Bahrain union. Other Gulf states protested Iran's "interference" in Bahraini affairs. It is shaping up to be another point of contention between the Sunni and Shi'a communities. Nobody seems to know what this union would actually look like, or how it would differ from the current Gulf Cooperation Council. Other Gulf states don't seem very excited about it but are open to continuing discussions. All Shi'a seem to agree that if it happens, it will be bad for them. They fear it will close the door to possible reform and will make it easier for the Saudis to intervene in Bahrain. The Sunnis point out that other regions have had greater benefits from integration and can't see why anyone wouldn't want to do it.

A few days ago I was playing at the swimming pool with my children and about ten other children from the neighborhood between the ages of five and ten. I was helping them have a "battle" where about five of them were in one raft and another five were in the other. One group would "attack" the other and try to tip over the inflatable raft, or they would jump onto the opposing raft and throw the others off. During one of the "attacks," a seven-year-old boy from a country in the region jumped from the raft into a group of attackers. Right before he jumped he yelled out, "I am going to sacrifice myself!" as he playfully threw his body into the attackers to fend off their attack. The language startled me. His family didn't seem especially religious, but it was clear he had picked up the idea that being a martyr for a good cause was an honorable thing. It was a stark reminder of the power of culture to shape one's thinking from an early age.

29 MAY 2012 (MOHAMMED)

Nabeel Rajab, the most recognized human rights activist, detained a few weeks ago, was released today. In his first statement, Rajab told his supporters that he promised to continue in his fight against the tyrannical regime until all Shi'a demands are met.

Zaynab Alkhawaja, the daughter of Abdulhadi Alkhawaja, released a statement today confirming that her father has stopped his hunger strike, which he began two months ago.

Violent Shi'a activity continued in area villages. On 28 May 2012, in Al-Dair, Shi'a burned tires in the vicinity of Bahrain International Airport sending a large smoke cloud into the sky.

In Sitra, the 14 February Youth Coalition continue to target Batelco communication hubs and network stations located in area villages. On 27 May 2012, Shi'a in Sitra targeted the Sitra police station with Molotov cocktails.

In Bani Jamra, Shi'a continue burning tires and blocking roads. On 27 May, Shi'a blocked the intersection near Country Mall with burned tires.

Shi'a in area villages also protested the latest sale of US arms to Bahrain. In Jidh Hafs, Sanabis, and Karbabad, Shi'a burned US flags and held a demonstration dominated by anti-US chanting.

3 JUNE 2012

Mehdi Hasan (@nsmehdihasan)
It saddens me how Sunnis want intervention in Syria & Shias want it in Bahrain. A bit more consistency & a bit less tribalism is much needed

Dima Khatib أنا ديمة (@Dima_Khatib)
Saudi FM : Looking at the number of victims in Syria and the number of victims in Bahrain, there is no comparison between the two situations

Ministry of Interior (@moi_bahrain)
A group of vandals burned tyres on Shaikh Isa bin Salman road. Police at the scene to secure and reopen the road #Bahrain

Nabeel Rajab (@NabeelRajab)
Attacking protesters with shotgun in many areas yesterday in #Bahrain including the capital Manama,where two people were attacked by shotgun

AlwefaqEN (@AlWefaqEN)
@WefaqGS : we support the peaceful way protesting and we do not approve of using the Molotov cocktails, #Bahrain

Eight people were convicted last week of plotting to overthrow the government, including attacking the Saudi Causeway and the Ministry of Interior building. They only received sentences of up to fifteen years, hinting to me that maybe the evidence again them was pretty thin or that the plotting they were allegedly engaged in was possibly less concrete anti-regime activity.

The Ministry of Interior stated that they have recovered over 8000 Molotov cocktails since the beginning of the year. This is the weapon of choice of the 14 February Youth Coalition, as well as that of related, more hard-line groups. They are so easy to make that it appears the government will be unable to stop their use. Their use also seems to be within the rules of the game, and is somewhat tolerated by the police.

Wefaq made a statement against the use of Molotov cocktails, but I doubt it will be heeded as those who use them follow other leaders.

Over the weekend, there were peaceful marches along Budaiyah Highway, with small-scale skirmishes occurring in several different areas. The government has started to erect tall fences along major roadways to make it more difficult for demonstrators to suddenly set up burning roadblocks.

My son told me a story about his recent visit to a neighbor from a Sunni country in the region. He said his friend's mom told him he couldn't go to the weekly swim class at the pool because they found out the teacher was Shi'a. No further explanation was necessary.

My children tell me that the Sunni children in the compound often tell them about the problems with the Shi'a, and how they are "the bad ones."

My friend, who is Shi'a, came over with his wife. They were excited to tell us that she is two months pregnant. We talked about the protests and the almost nightly use of tear gas in their village of Jidh Hafs. She was worried about the possible effect of the tear gas on her pregnancy, as there have been reports of Shi'a women having problems with their pregnancies because of the tear gas.

12 JUNE 2012

sosobahrain (@sosobahrain)
#Alwefaq #NabeelRajab stop using #children 2 clash with policemen 2 make a #media story! #bahrain

AlwefaqEN (@AlWefaqEN)
The security forces raided the house of Sheikh Ali Salman, Al Wefaq's GS on June 10, 2012 http://youtu.be/SCZRit2irn8 #Bahrain

Ministry of Interior (@moi_bahrain)
Interior Minister: Religious extremism is greatest internal threat which endanger Gulf security which Iran seeks to ferment

On Friday, a variety of Shi'a groups held marches along Budaiyah Highway that ended in some areas with tear gas and confrontations. The numbers were a little smaller than normal marches on Budaiyah Highway, possibly because of the rising heat or because there didn't seem to be senior religious leaders calling for widespread participation.

The leaders of Al-Wefaq have been encouraging people in clear terms not to use violence, and in some cases not to use Molotov cocktails against police. Al-Wefaq alleges that members of one of the security services attacked the outside of the home of its leader, Ali Salman. Perhaps as a result, he issued a statement asserting their resolve to continue pressing their demands. "The field marshal said 'if you come back, we will use two hundred percent more force,' but he should learn that the people are the source of power, and they have only used fifty percent so far."

A retired American police chief, John Timoney from Miami, made news by basically explaining that burning tires to draw police into Shi'a neighborhoods isn't a legitimate form of protest. He also added that when police are attacked in the course of responding to these roadblocks, they are justified in defending themselves. There may be some truth to police being justified in defending themselves when attacked, but I still remember driving past that demonstration in Sanabis. People were walking away, traffic was moving along, and it was only then that canisters of tear gas started falling all around us.

An eleven-year-old Shi'a boy, who was arrested for taking part in an illegal gathering, was released today pending his trial. His case made international news, as he was the youngest person arrested during the unrest. His lawyer said the police record reported that the police blamed him for some garbage they found in the road. These are the types of things that have a negative effect on the government's public relations effort. While I'm not sure what to do with an eleven-year-old demonstrator, it seems you could take action against the older ones first.

13 JUNE 2012 (MOHAMMED)

Ali Salman criticized the head of the Bahrain Defense Force (BDF), Ahmad Khalifa Bin Ahmad Al Khalifa, during a large rally a few days ago. As a result, he may be arrested, or at least asked to explain the comments he made. Salman said, directing his speech to the head of the BDF, that it would only take one fatwa for Shi'a to begin martyring themselves. King Hamad visited the BDF today, and in his comments, included an implied answer to Salman's threat, stating that anyone who does not respect the BDF is not a patriot and should be put to justice for their attacks on the BDF.

On 11 June 2012, during a confrontation with security forces, Shi'a in Al-Dair burned two armored vehicles. In Sitra, Shi'a continue to target Batelco communication centers by setting them on fire.

A new reconciliation society was formed to bridge the gap between Shi'a and Sunnis. The new society was endorsed by the crown prince. However, both Shi'a and Sunnis have little faith in this society, as the gap between them has increased significantly in the past year and half.

Al-Wafa al-Islami, the Islamic Action Society, and Haq Movement are organizing a joint event in the western province. This is the first joint event by the three extremist Shi'a groups since the uprising. The event will take place in Karzakan, Malkiya, Buri, and Damustan. The event is in support of Shi'a detainees and is supposed to take place on 16 June 2012.

18 JUNE 2012

S.Yousif Almuhafda (@SAIDYOUSIF)
Zahra(22yrs)arrested when participating n peaceful sit-in on Karbabad coast 15-6-12,beaten & her head scarf was forcibly removed #Bahrain"

Dominic Kavakeb (@DominicKavakeb)
They stole the eye of a 4 year old. For no reason. Even when #Bahrain is free, Ahmed will bare the scar of the regimes brutality

Jane Kinninmont (@janekinninmont)
Prince Nayef was seen as a driving force behind Saudi policy to Bahrain & Yemen (so close they're seen as partly interior ministry business)

Local press reported the seizure of large amounts of the materials used to make "high explosives" in area villages. The government seems to keep most incidents out of the media, but like to publicize their success in thwarting attacks. From early April to early May, there were a number of IEDs used at roadblocks. In the rest of May, there were many hoax IEDs placed at burning roadblocks. They seem to have backed away from this tactic, but the amount of chemicals and explosives seized suggests the demonstrators may be preparing for a change in strategy.

Saudi Crown Prince Nayef died a couple days ago. The King of Bahrain announced a three-day morning period, and now most radio stations are playing Islamic music and recitations. The Shi'a viewed him as part of the driving force behind the deployment of Saudi troops to Bahrain last year.

A friend of one of my neighbors displayed a hatred for the Shi'a that I have rarely seen first hand. She described them to me as animals that beat themselves in their religious processions and have no respect for human life. She had other horrible things to say about their religion. She said they take all the jobs and even monopolize the study-abroad programs. She said the guy in charge of foreign study grants is a Shi'a, and if he sees a Sunni name he just ignores it. Shi'a don't work, she said, and they expect to get everything for free. They are completely controlled by Iran and want Iran to take over the country. The protests in the City Centre Mall were a direct result of Barack Obama's call for negotiations with Wefaq. She disparaged Ali Salman and Isa Qassim. Isa Qassim told the Shi'a to kill Sunnis, she told me. I said, "Yes, I remember he said to 'crush them' if they see the police harming women. She said, "No, he just said to kill them." It has been a long time since I have encountered someone so far from reason that I felt no desire to offer any other perspective.

The leader of Wefaq, Ali Salman, made a speech where he said that with one word from their religious leader, they could bring tens of thousands to the streets and live their lives ready for death should it be necessary. He said they haven't yet brought half the intensity to the street that they are capable of. He said this in response to a military leader saying that if they tried to return to the Pearl Roundabout, they would face a much harder response than last time.

2 JULY 2012

Frank Gardner (@FrankRGardner)
UK sends police forensic detectives to #Bahrain to investigate huge find of bomb making materials.

Nabeel Rajab (@NabeelRajab)
The fence surrounding villages is a racist wall and building it is a bad decision - No to #apartheid wall in #Bahrain

Ministry of Interior (@moi_bahrain)
A group of thugs blocked Shaikh Khalifa bin Salman road with burning tyres. Police at the scene to reopen it #Bahrain

Ministry of Interior (@moi_bahrain)
The video presented in the press conference of the Chief of Public Security about High-Explosive Investigation http://www.youtube.com/watch?v=hTHycPyTS9o&feature=relmfu#Bahrain

The Bahrain police posted a video of the large amounts of chemicals and bomb-making materials they have seized in recent weeks. At the end of the video, they detonated some of the devices to show the explosive effects. One of them was set off in a car, and it completely destroyed the car. They seemed more powerful and sophisticated than bombs that have been used thus far.

Both authorized and unauthorized demonstrations occur almost daily. The unauthorized demonstrations usually quickly encounter a police response to disburse the crowd. There are several posted images of demonstrators wounded with bird shot. In some cases, it seems they were wounded as they aggressively approached the police. Many of the wounds are on their backs, suggesting they either turned around as the gun was aimed at them, or possibly they were already running away when they were shot. The fences around many of the major highways have made burning tires more difficult but in some instances, the demonstrators bring ladders and block the roads without too much difficulty.

I traveled to Jerusalem recently and had brief conversations about the situation in Bahrain with a few Palestinians. I was a little surprised by their lack of sympathy with the Shi'a opposition. They asked what the Bahraini Shi'a were unhappy about, and I mentioned a few things like the prime minister, and an unelected body that must approve laws passed by the Council of Representatives. They shrugged it off and said something about them probably never being satisfied. As the Palestinians were Sunni, I wondered how that might have affected their attitude towards the situation.

10 JULY 2012

Chan'ad Bahraini (@chanadbh)
Human Rights Watch: "If anyone is guilty of insult today, it is the Bahraini government" http://www.hrw.org/news/2012/07/11/bahrain-rights-activist-jailed-insulting-tweets #Bahrain

Yaser (@sorr0w)
Black smoke & burning tires can be seen everywhere! #Bahrain

Marc Owen Jones (@marcowenjones)
In the past year I've been insulted more times than in my entire life. No one was arrested for it though. I guess I'm not a town #Bahrain

Ministry of Interior (@moi_bahrain)
Saudi Interior Minister: Bahrain's security is part of Saudi Arabia's security & direct coordination between both countries is important

On 06 July, there was a large rally near the Burgerland Roundabout. Al-Wefaq led a march heading west on Budaiyah Highway while the 14 February Youth Coalition led a portion of the group in the other direction. The 14 February Youth Coalition at times takes advantage of authorized Al-Wefaq demonstrations to conduct their own demonstrations. Riot police were positioned all along Budaiyah Highway.

Nabeel Rajab was arrested again and sentenced to three months in jail for his Twitter posts. One of his tweets "insulted" the prime minister by saying people living in Muharraq were only supporting him for financial gain. His arrest makes it look like there is no freedom of expression in Bahrain, which will likely only help the opposition portray the government in a negative light. However, last week, fifteen policemen were charged with abusing prisoners, scoring the government some points for following through with the BICI recommendations and showing a desire to hold people accountable for violating human rights.

The government officially banned the Islamic Action Society, a.k.a. "Amal," and cited a number of violations to support their decision, such as meeting in religious buildings, failing to submit a budget, and not holding a convention in the past four years. The real reason for the decision is likely Amal's hard-line stance, seeking major reforms. This will not have a major impact on things, as they will likely continue to meet, but it may drive them further away from working within the law.

A few blocks from the American Navy base in Juffair, roads have regularly been blocked at night. It is usually only ten to twenty youth who have brief skirmishes with police after they block the roads, leaving "American Alley," a street with numerous fast food restaurants. A few days ago they blocked the road in front of the Bahrain School, a school with a lot of American students. The burning roadblock also had a hoax explosive device that caused the police to keep the road closed for longer than normal. Social media continues to show aggressive attacks against police with Molotov cocktails and operations to block roads around the country.

20 JULY 2012

Mohamed Mustafa (@MoMustafaMD)

Thought the #bahrain timeline might be a bit different in Ramadan. Nope.

AlwefaqEN (@AlWefaqEN)

Watch "English report: 72 areas subjected to brutal suppression by Bahrain regime forces" on YouTube -http://www.youtube.com/watch?v=rPtYe23iBJg&feature=youtube_gdata_player #Bahrain

S.Yousif Almuhafda (@SAIDYOUSIF)

several protests in different parts of #bahrain being attacked by riot police now

Ministry of Interior (@moi_bahrain)

Incidents in Bahrain were not internal matters since they received outside support to escalate them to the level of violence and vandalism

Ministry of Interior (@moi_bahrain)

Interior Minister during his visit to US: Bahrain leads the way to a democratic approach since the launch of reform project by HM the King

In many different areas today, there were protests against a government plan to ban protests and marches. News media highlighted protests in Diraz (where Sheikh Isa Qassim resides and preaches) and Musalla, but similar demonstrations occurred in at least ten different areas. Government forces moved to disperse the crowds, and several people were wounded by bird shot. There were numerous instances of a handful of protestors attacking the police with Molotov cocktails. The protests have only been a minor disruption to life in Bahrain. This measure only adds fuel to their anger and is another item on their list of grievances against the government. It will also likely drive more people to think cooperation with the government is futile. Just when the opposition starts to lose a little steam, the government always seems to step up, giving something new to be angry about.

31 JULY 2012

AlwefaqEN (@AlWefaqEN)

Gangs of darkness usually undertake night attacks on houses spreading terror and horror in neighbourhoods #DarknessGangs

Sayed Yousif Shehab (@SayedYousif)

Horrific injuries in Sitra past night. Why Western countries roll red carpet for torturers. #Bahrain @MSF_USA @msf_uk

IAA Bahrain (@IAA_Bahrain)
Press Release: Ministry of Interior Announces Investigation into Allegations of Police Misconduct http://ow.ly/czEwH #Bahrain

Two days ago as I prepared to make a right turn onto Juffair Avenue, I saw cars making abrupt U-turns, and several others scrambling off the road to drive onto a dirt lot. I quickly saw that the road ahead had been blocked with police cars and tape. The police had blocked the road because of a protest and roadblock that included a couple of canisters that they thought might be bombs. The road was reopened about an hour later.

Neither Ramadan nor the extreme heat has slowed down the protest activity. There are regular protests, often in support of a specific grievance such as prisoners or a recent decision by the government. By not authorizing demonstrations, the government makes it more likely that the protests that do occur will be less controlled, and more likely to be led by groups willing to engage in violence against the police. Negotiations are blocked because of preconditions set by both sides. The recent raids on bomb-making factories and the few arrests are ominous signs. There was a front-page article in a local paper saying 1,500 people, including Bahraini, are being trained by Iran and Hezbollah in Iraq. While this information was likely fabricated or at least exaggerated, it shows how the government continues to characterize the protest movement as terrorists serving foreign interests.

4 AUGUST 2012

Gloria (@gloriahere)
.@RepWyden .@RepMcGovern Tell me would we tolerate this here in #USA ???? 700 'policemen hurt this year' http://www.gulf-daily-news.com/NewsDetails.aspx?storyid=335077 #Bahrain

Ahmed Hussain Allen (@iridwial)
700 Police hurt since beginning of the year by terrorist attacks http://is.gd/HX0QtJ What terrorists? How many civilians killed? #Bahrain

In a statement to the Human Rights Commission, US Assistant Secretary of State Michael Posner praised the Bahraini government for setting up the Bahrain Independent Commission of Inquiry. He stated that violence had dropped significantly and that there "are signs of the government's commitment to address the underlying cause of last year's violence," he noted. Many people here, who see the daily attacks on police, view this announcement with skepticism. Moreover, the recent statement by the Ministry of Interior that over seven hundred policemen have been injured since the start of the year also contradicts that finding. I think Secretary Posner confuses the progress the government is making in reforming the security services, with the underlying issue of the Shi'a seeking a more representative government, which demand those in power have shown very little interest in accommodating.

Police are posted every kilometer or so along major roads to intervene in case of attempted roadblocks. Social networking sites described a police bus that was attacked with Molotov cocktails near Bani Jamra and numerous arrests in that area. The couple of kilometers of highway nearest the Saudi Causeway were resurfaced. I wondered if it was to cover up all the burn damage on the road so people entering the country wouldn't be concerned about what was going on.

There continue to be complaints about large numbers of police raids at night to arrest those involved in the unrest. Bahrain is such a small country that if you detain enough people, it really could affect the numbers involved in the "unauthorized protests." However, widespread arrests could increase the number of people who want to be actively involved in the unrest and drive some segments of the opposition to consider more aggressive methods.

11 AUGUST 2012

Mohammed AlMaskati (@emoodz)
Looks like we're going to have an active week ahead, protests announced on the 12th, 14th and the 17th marking various occasions.. #Bahrain

Khalid Ibrahim (@khalidibrahim12)

19 Members of the #US Congress call on the king of #Bahrain to release Nabeel Rajab and all other prisoners of conscious.

Saeed Shehabi (@SaeedShehabi)

US,UK must realise they are betting on losing horse. They are better advised to side with people, not dictators. Regime indefensible

Fatima (@TamtoomHalwachi)

The situation is horrible in #Aali heavy crackdown on protest, attacking women arresting&torturing youth along with house raids! #Bahrain

Sectarian tensions have flared up somewhat in recent days. The Shi'a have had religious gatherings in remembrance of the death of Iman Ali and to celebrate "the Night of Al-Qadr." At an event in Muharraq this week, a Sunni group attacked a Shi'a gathering.

There have been some meetings between Bahraini officials and several opposition leaders. It didn't appear any progress was made—just the opposite, the meetings seemed to add more conditions to having serious discussions. The Justice Minister said, "They [opposition groups] must take clear and definitive positions, without giving any political cover to criminal acts."

Roads continue to be blocked around the country, normally in Shi'a neighborhoods, but sometimes major highways. Street battles with police occurred in Sitra, Aali, among other areas. Police on foot patrol in Bani Jamra were attacked with Molotov cocktails, severely burning a policeman.

22 AUGUST 2012

S.Yousif Almuhafda (@SAIDYOUSIF)

#Bahrain A number of women and children suffocated and got injured after riot police attacked the mourners of martyr Husam Al-Haddad"

Ministry of Interior (@moi_bahrain)
A video shows rioting and vandalism after a funeral in Muharraq http://bit.ly/SiBK8m

Sayed Yousif Shehab (@SayedYousif)
Several casualties reported by HRDs from many areas across #Bahrain, caused by #UK shotguns, treated @ homes. @msf_UK http://pic.twitter.com/E0A6HiFr

Bahrain announced it would reinstate its ambassador to Iran. The government recalled him last March, after Iran criticized its treatment of the demonstrators. Iran responded to this by saying it would not resend its ambassador to Bahrain as long as the Bahraini government continues to abuse its citizens.

There were nightly clashes with police in several different areas in Bahrain this week. The use of shotguns by the police seems more prevalent. One protestor from the mixed Sunni and Shi'a area of Muharraq died from a shotgun wound, and there were intense engagements with police after his funeral this week. The prime minister attempted to quell the sectarian tensions by saying, "The spirit of coexistence shown by the people of Muharraq is a model which characterises the people of Bahrain." He added, "No one can fuel divisions among the people of Muharraq."

People have reported hearing propane tanks exploding much more frequently this week. There have even been a few instances of pipe bombs being used in conjunction with burning roadblocks, including one not too far from the McDonalds in Tubli, in the area of the American Embassy.

4 SEPTEMBER 2012

[US] Department of State (@StateDept)
U.S. urges #Bahrain to abide by its commitment to right to due process and to transparent judicial proceedings. http://go.usa.gov/rmvB

Ahmed Bin Mohamed (@ba7rain_vip)
To the outsiders helping shia'a terrorists in #Bahrain stop looking @ Things by one eye.there are people more than the ones you support.

Carl Bildt (@carlbildt)
I'm very worried by new heavy sentencing of protesters in Bahrain. This is not the way to achieve reconciliation and a good society.

Ministry of Interior (@moi_bahrain)
A group of thugs blocked Shaikh Isa bin Salman road with burning tyres. Police at the scene to reopen it.

This morning the court confirmed the prison sentences of the twenty opposition leaders who were arrested after last year's uprising. Eight of them have life sentences. The statement added that they had contact with Hezbollah and other external organizations (i.e., Iran). There was a lot of commentary about how this was meant as a sign of firmness by the government. The Shi'a opposition was furious and promised widespread protests.

Today I was coming home from an evening school activity when the cars in front of me came to a sudden stop. I could see thick black smoke rising fiercely across the highway. Cars maneuvered slowly to move into a better position with some hoping they might be able to move to one side or the other to get around. Police cars struggled to pass along the side. About ten guys in civilian clothes went running past my car, carrying some type of gun, either shotguns or tear gas guns. A few seconds later a few other guys walked past wearing yellow police vests. A few seconds later, a tear gas canister was fired off in the general direction of the Shi'a village of Saar. A car behind me started honking, and I moved forward a little—as much as I could. A few seconds later, someone banged on the back of my car, yelling for me to move. I then saw he had a police light placed on the top of his SUV. After I moved over a little he got out again to tell the people in front on me to move over. I thought it was funny that he was wearing an old T-shirt that said, "An Army of One," a slogan for the US Army. It looked like a T-shirt that he just happened to be wearing that day. It took the police about twenty minutes to put out the fires (mainly made out of tires). More and more police arrived: the riot police, the traffic police, the EOD (bomb crew), the crime scene truck, and so on, all in a variety of different vehicles. The police eventually tried to get the cars to back up, which was amusing since the traffic was probably backed up for kilometers. There was a "device" the bomb squad was looking at. They took pictures of it, and then put it into evidence bags. I could see it, since I was only a few cars away from the whole scene. It was a fire hydrant attached with a wire to some sort of box.

When they finally let us pass about an hour later, I could see the other side of the highway was blocked because the same thing was happening there. I could see a guy in a protective bomb suit working on some device. I later heard this happened in several different areas around the island. I later found out the device blocking my road was a hoax, but it served its purpose of prolonging the roadblock, because real IEDs have wounded numerous policemen in the past making them hesitant to approach the devices.

When I picked my son up from school yesterday I paused as I saw a lady and a child run toward the entrance beside me. I let her enter first and she apologized, explaining about how all the burning roadblocks along the way had made her late to pick up her son. I hear different reports of what some people call improvised explosive devices (IEDs), both real and hoax, being placed in different areas around the island. You hear about propane tanks being used more frequently and even pipe bombs, normally in Shi'a areas. Some of the hoaxes have been found in commercial areas, causing people to wonder what would happen if one actually went off in such a place. Right before I went to bed, I heard an explosion in the distance that slightly rattled my windows. It was probably a propane tank exploding no further than a kilometer away.

5 SEPTEMBER 2012

Ministry of Interior (@moi_bahrain)

A terror act on Budaiyah highway near Deraz that targeted on-duty policemen, 2 of them injured & 2 police jeeps and 2 cars of Bahrainis damaged

6 SEPTEMBER 2012

Yaser (@sorr0w)
Now in AlSanabis, police are everywhere in the alleyways chasing us, a house might got raided just now. #Bahrain

شبكة ستر الخارجية (@kharjiyanews)
Bahrain: Now riot police attacking protesters by shotgun without mercy in sitra alkharjiya village #bh #sitra #14feb

14 SEPTEMBER 2012

Maryam Alkhawaja (@MARYAMALKHAWAJA)
Huge protest in #Bahrain today demanding democracy, wasn't violent or about movie so u prolly won't hear abt it on the news

Joanne Michele (@sabzbrach)
Meanwhile in Bahrain, they're protesting against their own government. How much media coverage do you think that will get?

Kety Shapazian (@KetyDC)
Mosques have been destroyed in Bahrain and noone in the Middle East protested against this.

Toby C. Jones (@tobycraigjones)
Who's not protesting at the US Embassy in #Bahrain? Pro-democracy opposition. Who is? Regime's crazy radical base. US has great friends

Mohammed AlMaskati (@emoodz)
Repost: Flags of AlQaeda waved during a protest stand in the proximity of the American Embassy in #Bahrain v @Bu7asan_

The region was shocked by the attack on the US Consulate in Benghazi, Libya, that killed four US government employees.

There were also large demonstrations in Cairo and Yemen, and then the next day, there were more in a number of other Muslim countries. Everyone was wondering about what would happen here, and how the protests would spread throughout the region. The protests were prompted by a film insulting Islam's founder, Mohammed, made by an Egyptian Christian living in California. Both Sunni and Shi'a leaders called for demonstrations today outside mosques.

A demonstration planned for last night outside the US Embassy didn't occur. The Ministry of the Interior (MOI) announced that they would use force to prevent it from happening. It is hard to tell how much the warning and security presence deterred the protestors. I've driven past the embassy several times over the past three days and there always seemed to be a few extra SUVs around, once a MOI bus with riot police onboard, and later in the evening, I saw a couple of the new armored vehicles they have used since last February. I saw a photo on the Internet about a small demonstration held across the street from the embassy. The event was simply a small group making a statement, with the Islamic flags used by Al-Qaeda and other Sunni fundamentalists in the background.

I visited my friend Ali today, whom I had not seen in a couple months. I awkwardly told him I was sorry about the video, and how I thought it was a terrible thing. He told me not to worry about it. He said people can distinguish between the American government and the American people, and that all the Americans he has known have been great. I found it ironic he used this common saying in the Middle East in this instance. Logic would say that the protestors at the embassy are unable to distinguish between the actions of a small group of Americans who produced the movie, and the American government. Normally this phrase is used when talking about US military actions or other policy decisions. In this case, it was an American citizen who had been at fault, and yet the American government was paying the price. Perhaps in many Middle Eastern countries a movie like this could not be produced without the government's approval. I responded that in this case it wasn't even the US government's fault, but I think the point was lost because of our language barrier.

I drove down Budaiyah Highway as a demonstration was concluding. I saw only part of the crowd as they dispersed, but there were over a thousand people walking past my car as I slowly moved closer to the Saar/Barbar Roundabout. Some held photos of detained Shi'a activists; some had Bahraini flags tied around their shoulders like capes. I had heard that a US flag had been burned earlier in the day not too far from there, so I was mildly cautious about my Western face drawing attention.

There seems to be misunderstanding about the situation all around me. My neighbors from South Asia seemed to have no idea what the Shi'a protestors were upset about. I gave them a basic overview as they vented how frustrated they were to miss a religious function. The guard at our housing compound told me the Shi'a only want to get paid and not have to work. He repeated, "How can that be, that people would expect to get money without having to work?" I didn't bother trying to unravel the complexities of the conflict.

The deaths from the attack on the consulate in Benghazi came as a shock to people in my office. It made me think about why the news of some deaths affects people more than others. One guy in my office was so angry he seemed to purposely accuse Islam of causing so many problems in the world, even though a Muslim co-worker was in the room. He said something like, "Almost every problem in the world, from the Phillippines, South Asia, all the way to North Africa…anywhere where Islam is, it brings problems." They debated a little, and I stayed out of it because of the emotion involved, but I told my Muslim co-worker that it was too bad the actions of extremists in Libya was being used to discredit the whole religion.

21 SEPTEMBER 2012

AlwefaqEN (@AlWefaqEN)
Regime forces turn the Capital Manama into a war zone #bahrain

Bahrain (@mowalee)
#Bahrain | Armored vehicles n the capital #Manama & close roads by d MOI disrupts d interests of d citizens & hurt the economy

ديفيدسون كريستوفر [Christopher Davidson] (@dr_davidson)
Fresh clashes in #Bahrain as protestors move demonstrations closer to
the heart of the capital city:

People are still on edge as protests against the anti-Islam film continue in many countries across the Muslim world. A French maga-
zine published some insulting cartoons about Mohamed, which only
added fuel to the fire. There have been a variety of small protests
across Bahrain, but nothing too significant. Other protests included
sentiments about the film, even if that wasn't the focus of the gatherings. My neighbor from a French-speaking country talked about the
concern the French community had about violence or protests against
their schools or embassy. She also said it was really unfortunate that
people felt the need to create or publish things like these cartoons,
were obviously intended to infuriate people.

Every night there are small, unauthorized demonstrations, blocked
roads, and attacks on policemen. One recent newspaper article talked
about the hundreds of injured policemen in the past year. As much as they
can be criticized for using force to disrupt "unauthorized demonstrations,"
they have shown an amazing amount of restraint in the face of attacks
by young Shi'a. No doubt in most Western nations, if a group of masked
young men ran at policemen, they would be immediately met with lethal
force. However, this restraint is probably the one thing that is keeping tensions in Bahrain from becoming more like the situation in Syria.

Tonight there was a large Shi'a gathering in the Manama Souq
area. It was considered an unauthorized demonstration, and there were
rumors that the protestors were going to try to march along the main
road back to the Pearl Roundabout (now called the Farouq Junction).
It seems the government completely shut down the highways leading
into the area to contain the size of the demonstration, and then tear
gassed, arrested, and otherwise disrupted the attendees.

Five men were charged with attempted murder for an attack several months ago on policemen in the Shi'a village, Diraz. The policemen responded to a burning roadblock and were ambushed when they
arrived. This is the most serious charge brought against people who
have attacked the police since the period of unrest in February and
March last year.

Seven policemen were also charged this week for torturing detained protestors and forcing them to sign confessions. This will probably have some deterrent effect on other policemen and may have a slight negative impact on the morale of the police force. It will probably also help a little in the public diplomacy arena, but will not have a noticeable impact on the opinion of Shi'a here in Bahrain.

23 SEPTEMBER 2012

ArabianBusiness.com (@ArabianBusiness)
Bahrain eyes Smurfs theme park to revive tourism: Bahrain is aiming to reignite its tourism sector after months ... http://bit.ly/PMA8SA

Mazen Mahdi (@MazenMahdi)
According to authorities 29 people had been detained for the Manama protests earlier and referred to Public Prosecution #Bahrain

My wife called me yesterday while she was on her way to a birthday party for our daughter. She was stopped in traffic on Budaiyah Highway for about forty-five minutes because of a burning roadblock in front of her. She saw the black, billowing smoke finally slowly die down, and then the traffic eventually started moving again. I told her to stay in the car, rather than giving into curiosity and trying to see if they were making any progress.

I had a discussion with a friend today about what would happen in Bahrain if Israel attacked Iran. He thought that Iran would immediately launch missiles at the US Navy Base here. I told him it could easily escalate to that point, but that I thought at first they would avoid trying to bring America into the fight and would try to focus their immediate response on punishing Israel as severely as they could. I was surprised to come home and see that an IRGC official had said, "Whether the Zionist regime attacks with or without US knowledge, then we will definitely attack US bases in Bahrain, Qatar, and Afghanistan." They frequently seem to say things for shock and possibly for their deterrent value, but I wonder if they really mean this. Either way, things will likely be difficult for Westerners, especially Americans, if that war kicks off.

When I explained a few things from the Shi'a perspective, my wife asked me how I could support them when they follow Iran, who are the enemies of the West. I explained that if reform happens in a peaceful, negotiated way, the outcome probably wouldn't be against the interests of Western countries. However, if the radicals, who are more closely allied with Iran, are strengthened by a lack of progress, eventually succeed in ending the current system, their position in the new government will be more pronounced. I explained that while Arab Spring democracy has exposed the risks of democracy, I still believed Bahrain could find an agreement that would be in everyone's interest, even for the Al Khalifas, who may be able to preserve a form of a monarchy without the chaos going on in the streets.

29 SEPTEMBER 2012

Ministry of Interior (@moi_bahrain)
A terror act targeted on-duty policemen lives when a huge number of terrorists hurled Molotov cocktails at them in Sadad #Bahrain

AlwefaqEN (@AlWefaqEN)
The regime forces in #Bahrain killed Ali Neama(17yro), with birdshot at close range,while pro-democracy protests took to streets.

S.Yousif Almuhafda (@SAIDYOUSIF)
#Bahrain tens of thousands in the furenal are chanting down with king hamad

AnarchistBH (@AnarchistBH)
Regime targets a child with pellets to his back, bled to death! then they say "#Bahrain on the brink of a new era"

My wife and I were returning together from the area near the Bahrain International Circuit and were stopped at a police checkpoint. As soon as he saw my wife's blond hair, he motioned for us to go ahead. I found out later that a funeral march, for a seventeen-year-old boy who had been killed by police yesterday, was being held close to that area in Hamad Town. As we drove home, we saw a few different columns of black smoke in the distance, off the main highway. Some say the fact that his lethal wounds from a shotgun (bird shot) were in the back is proof that the government is massacring innocent protestors. I'll admit, it doesn't look good, especially in the international media. However, in order to die from bird shot, you have to be pretty close to the shooter. In most of the cases I have seen, the police fire bird shot when someone runs at them with Molotov cocktails or some other weapon. It is possible that he ran close to the police, and threw something like a Molotov cocktail, and as the police aimed to fire, he turned to run away. It will be hard to know for sure, but either way, it is a significant loss to the government in the public- and international-opinion battle. A few hundred protestors broke off from the funeral march and skirmished with the police in the usual way. As usual, social media comments portrayed this as the police attacking the funeral.

In the early morning, I ran some errands and came across a group of about six riot police SUVs across the road. As I approached, I could see there was a serious car accident, and it looked like one of the police cars had crashed into the back of a car with a family in it. No one appeared to be hurt, but I imagined it happening as the police car was rushing to respond to the latest disruption.

A few days ago, I was driving a co-worker who was visiting from another country back to her hotel. It was her first time in the Middle East. We were stuck in traffic as the sun was setting. Suddenly, a thick column of smoke rose high in the sky from a point about eight cars in front of us. I didn't wait to see the response and quickly made a sharp U-turn before other cars also starting trying to move off in odd directions and the traffic situation became ugly. It ended up taking us about a half an hour longer to get to her hotel.

8 OCTOBER 2012

BeladOnlineEng & frn (@BeladOnlineEng)

Bahrain had a disasterous week. Martyr after martyr. Medics back in prison. Zainab beaten up. Nabeels mum died. We MUST #SaveNabeelRajab

TheTwoSeas (@TheTwoSeas)
Nabeel Rajab weaker on third day of hunger strike following mother's funeral http://bit.ly/QYvq6v #Bahrain #SaveNabeelRajab

Gloria (@gloriahere)
We want to live peacefully in #Bahrain Yet #nabeelrajab terrorists attempt to harm innocent civilians! http://youtu.be/zdhxdQ7fadU via @someo1n

Ministry of Interior (@moi_bahrain)
Two private cars damaged when groups of lawbreakers attacked policemen with Molotov cocktails on Shaikh Isa Al Kabeer road

المحرق أحرار (@J_Ashabi)
Urgent: thousands of protesters of #Bahrain are walking straight to the Pearl Roundabout "Center of The Revolution"

This past week, the unrest has been going very strong, with something happening every few days that adds fuel to the fire. Every night there are about eight to ten different burning roadblocks and several police vehicles are attacked with Molotov cocktails. A few police cars have been burned, and several police have been wounded by a few real IEDs, including one in Eker, near Sitra.

Mohammed Mushayma died at Salmaniya Hospital while undergoing treatment for sickle cell anemia. He was in custody, serving a seven-year sentence. This, following the death of Ali Nemaa, really angered the Shi'a population, and some even made an attempt to retake the Pearl Roundabout. One of my friends said she saw between fifty and a hundred police vehicles, along with several hundred policemen, in the area of the Pearl Roundabout before the expected march. The marchers were dispersed, but a few police vehicles were destroyed in the process.

My son asked me what some graffiti meant on the wall: "We Won Freedom," it read. I said they probably meant to write, "We Want Freedom." My son said that it doesn't help their cause if they can't spell right. I said the fact that it is written in English was the most important thing. It shows they want the outside world to understand what they are striving for. Of course, it could have been spelled right, and the writer thinks the protestors have already won.

I saw my Shi'a friend Ali again, and he told me his wife's pregnancy is going well. He lives in a village near Bilad al-Qadeem. He said whenever they are having a big demonstration, he takes his wife to visit relatives in another area so she doesn't put the baby at risk by inhaling the tear gas. We talked about the situation, and he denied the Shi'a ever use real bombs. I told him they weren't big bombs, but that still, simple, improvised bombs have wounded some policemen. He said the Shi'a would never do it because the police would come down too hard on them. I guess some things are easier to see from the outside looking in. I asked his wife later what they planned to name the baby. "Hussein," she said, reminding me how the cultural and religious legacy of a religion is transmitted through the centuries.

16 OCTOBER 2012

M. K. Al-Binateej (@ATEEKSTER)
#Bahrain AntiGov rioters placed a suspicious package on Sh.Khalifa highway & burned tires going towards #Manama

Alwefaq Society (@ALWEFAQ)
Talks of dialogue and political resolution are of no credibility

AlwefaqEN (@AlWefaqEN)
Sheikh Isaa Qassim talkes about how the authority exploits "crush him" #Bahrain read his Friday sermon: http://alwefaq.net/index.php?show=news&action=article&id=7083 …

abdulnabi alekry (@anhalekry)
What on earth #Bahrain police interrogate Ali Salman head of#WEFAQ largest legal opposition party for visiting Egypt farce democracy

الخياط خالد [Khalid Al-Khayat] (@KhalidAlkhayat)
#Felix handed over his Jump Cert 2#Ali_Salman:U deserve it more than me! U R much better jumper!U jump over ur own ppl blood & soul!#Bahrain

Yesterday, police questioned the Secretary General of Al-Wefaq, Ali Salman, about his recent trip to Egypt. He said there wasn't a revolution going on in Bahrain like other Arab Spring countries, and that the people just wanted reforms and a constitutional monarchy. He was criticized by some of the other opposition groups for backing away from their hopes of a complete revolution.

Two days ago, my family and I were driving through a neighborhood, slowly moving through the traffic. A group of about twelve police in riot gear slowly walked past the car. A couple of minutes later, they came walking towards us again, and many of them looked at us cautiously as they passed us by.

Last Friday, there were a number of demonstrations in the Manama Souq area. The protesters seemed to do better with the advantage of the small streets, which allowed them to avoid the police response, especially compared to the wide open areas of the Pearl Roundabout area. Demonstrations continue nightly with tire-burnings and Molotov cocktails thrown at police. Hoax bombs and small IEDs are still used every few days. Usually the hoax bombs are used along with the roadblocks, and the real ones are usually used in an open area in a Shi'a village, occasionally intending to injure the police. While the unrest continues nightly, there still does not appear to be any sign the government is going to break down and make any concessions.

The leading Shi'a cleric in Bahrain, Isa Qassim, has come under pressure for some of his recent statements that seemed to justify violence against the government. Here's a translation—taken directly from alewfaq.net—of part of his speech last Friday, where he addressed this topic:[xv]

This is the logic of the unilateral authority. On the contrary, the logic of the peoples who are longing for freedom, and longing to get their right to self-determination. That is the logic of reason, conscience and religion and the logic of all international covenants, it's the kind of logic that is only rejected by an oppressive ideology.

The peoples are neither violent nor vindictive, and it has been so clear that all Arab-Spring revolutions started as peaceful movements. The authorities' violence and over-killing pulled some revolutions into violence to face their authority's abortion of freedom through the people's bloodshed.

The peaceful popular movement of the people of Bahrain presented a good example of adhering to the peaceful approach, this embarrassed the authorities that are trying recklessly to drag the people into violence in order to escape entitlements of the people's rights.

In Bahrain, there is a peaceful movement for reform. The people of Bahrain demand a

- constitution that guarantees the will of the people , and

- fair distribution of electoral constituencies,

- a fairly elected house of representative (parliament)

- elected government

- a non-politicized independent judiciary

- Equality without any kind of discrimination in all state

  departments

Is there a nation that in this region or the whole world that denies such legitimate demands? Or are the Bahraini people excluded from this world and should not have the right to demand their rights? Don't they have right to democracy.

The people of Bahrain is one of the peoples that have the same rights of other peoples in the world, the authority is practicing unjustifiable violence against the people of Bahrain, and this has embarrassed it in front of the world."

The authority in Bahrain is practicing unjustifiable violence and terror against peaceful people calling for legitimate demands which cannot be denied by anyone. This oppressive situations is embarrassing the regime in front of the international community and human rights organizations, when the issue of Bahrain is internationally discussed, however the authority is in desperate need of justifications for its violence against the legitimate popular demands.

The regime is trying relentlessly to find an excuse for its violence, that is why we find it

- lying publically in the media

- always trying to link the popular movement to a foreign plot

- creating fake speeches and relating them to religious and political figures, claiming that they call for violence despite their repeated pronounce calls for peaceful movement.

However, they make fake sound clips by cutting out a part of a footage and using the sentences or words according to their plot that aims to damage the image of the peaceful movement, and any figure or party that stands by it. This mission aims mainly to falsely relate calls for violence a particular person or party, with no shame or conscience.

The state media has cut out "Crush him" from its context which called for legitimate defense (for women), it has been repeatedly said by state officials and deliberately focused on (alone) to mislead the public inside and outside Bahrain, without shame in such a scandalous obvious lie.

This goes on as a large number of are victimized and killed by the security forces, yet, the authority approves such behavior justifying it as self-defense! So there is an obliged and permissible self-defense which is initial-killing, while a call to defend women is terror? Here, I am asking any minister, official, cleric, journalist. What will he do if his family was attacked? Will the minister let anyone come close to attacking females of his family?

The authority escalated its violence level, from time to time, to deal with the popular movement in a way may bring violence on streets so as to serve as pretext in order to smash the movement in one strike.

The authority is longing for a call for violence from a political association or a cleric that stand by the people in their demands, in order to meet its desired purpose to strike a justifiable crushing blow against the opposition. These kind of calls won't be adopted by an association, a cleric nor any pro-justice and pro-reform Friday sermon.

Personally, it is impossible for me to call for violence neither directly nor indirectly. My religion is my deterrent, I cannot accept violence against Muslims and all humanity. Also, my love for this valuable homeland, and my interest of its safety and its citizens' security keep me far from adopting such irrational speech. Slandering, defamation, abuse, threats and menaces aiming to stop the Friday prayers; or even what is recently understood as death threats from one of the journalist when he included such threats in his article, recently, stating that "If the State will not take its right from (Isa), the people are capable to do so."

The authority's message has been received. But, defending rights of people is a humanitarian responsibility that a religious person will not turn his back on. All offenses and threats will not make me disvalue the blood of the people, and I will not call for violence.

The authority is also longing for this tribune and others to become a source of sectarian calls that spark war fire between brothers who share religion, homeland and destiny. This war may burn anyone, and therefore the people are requested then to give in to the unjust authority which will enjoy full and complete power. It is impossible for this tribune to serve for such desires of the authority. We will fight such sectarian ideologies and will work to abort any attempt to play with fire.

There is no doubt that the authority has the required power and ability to stop the Friday sermons, and all other sermons, as it had threatened. However, it will be impossible for that to go on. The people will not be silenced, and will continue to demand for their right to real reform. Such tyrannical acts will only bring more people to believe that this authority is an oppressive one.

The people's political awareness, their will and determination to peacefully get their rights, will not be affected by denying a cleric freedom of opinion, or closing a mosque here or there. Are the people going to back-down if a particular cleric kept silent? This is complete illusion.

This tribune had always had a fixed stance regarding the political issue and popular movement in Bahrain. This tribune will always stand by the people in their legitimate demands and their right to peaceful movement until their demands are met. We will not stand by terror and will not stand by the oppressive government with all its pronounced terror. We will always call for peaceful movement and real reform.

22 OCTOBER 2012

Ministry of Interior (@moi_bahrain)
Chief of Public Security: policeman died on Friday morning as a result of a bomb explosion & seriously injured a second police officer #BAH

sosobahrain (@sosobahrain)
The reason of police checkpoints in #AlEker is to find the criminals who killed policeman by bomb on Thursday #bahrain

AlwefaqEN (@AlWefaqEN)
special forces deployed in Sitra to suppress peaceful pro-democracy unarmed citizens. !!!! #Bahrain pic.twitter.com/i63WLHVI

Ministry of Interior (@moi_bahrain)
Central Police Director: security measures in Ekar are to search for wanted suspects http://www.policemc.gov.bh/en/news_details.aspx?type=1&articleId=15084 ...

Ministry of Interior (@moi_bahrain)
We won't stop at just who committed the crime, but also determine who orchestrated the explosion and who trained the individuals#Bahrain

Maryam Alkhawaja (@MARYAMALKHAWAJA)
MOI 1st said: terrorist bombing then: metal rod projector now: bombing again, locals say cmpltely diff story cont #bahrain #aleker

S.Yousif Almuhafda (@SAIDYOUSIF)
#Bahrain Urgent appeal: Medical supplies and food needed in AlEkerhttp://bahrainrights.hopto.org/en/node/5487 #Humanrights

On Friday night, a policeman was killed in Eker, a Shi'a neighborhood near Sitra. The policemen were patrolling through the neighborhood and were attacked with Molotov cocktails and some other IED that caused a lethal head injury to one Pakistani in the Bahrain police force, and put another policeman in critical condition. The police have put checkpoints in place around the village in order to find those involved in the attack. Some social media sites say that other demonstrations have flared up in an attempt to divert police away from Eker, and there are even reports of groups marching to Eker to help "lift the siege."

Other activity, including violent attacks against police and burning tires, continues to occur throughout Bahrain, although mostly in Shi'a neighborhoods. Outdoor protest activity tends to fluctuate somewhat because of the weather, and it is starting to cool down. I hear different stories from friends and neighbors about what they see out on the roads, and everyone seems to notice the increase in activity. There is a steady stream of news about both police and demonstrators being charged with a variety of illegal acts, and then how both communities react to the accusations. Probably in response to Isa Qassim's speech, I read an article warning that it is prohibited to use religious venues to make political speeches.

24 OCTOBER 2012

S. Yousif Almuhafda (@SAIDYOUSIF)

Security forces using pellet shotguns in attacks on protests in Bani Jamrah and Duraz, reports that there r a number of wounded

Saqer S Al Khalifa (@SaqerAlKhalifa)

I personally don't think that acts shown in this video have anything to do with pro-democracy. #Bahrain

IFEX (@IFEX)

#Bahraini justice minister threatens to use "coercive force" against opposition clerics

Last night my wife drove past Diraz, a Shi'a village along Budaiyah Highway. She said there were about twenty police SUVs lined up along the road, with about a hundred police standing in their riot gear on both sides of the road, looking away from the road. There were several little fires scattered around the area that could have been the remnants of Molotov cocktails burning out. I found out later that several protestors were severely wounded last night by bird shot. This wasn't a regular protest. I've seen hundreds of videos of these encounters and normally someone is shot when they get too close to the police with a Molotov cocktail. The government may be to blame for not authorizing more demonstrations, and using tear gas and stun grenades to disperse protestors, but I've only heard of the police using bird shot when lethal force is directed at them.

Tonight, I was driving to Saar with my two boys. As we approached Saar Avenue, we saw a column of smoke in the horizon. Soon enough we saw cars going in reverse, driving in the wrong direction, the other direction, U-turning…a total free-for-all. I continued and saw a fierce fire raging, completely covering the road from wall to wall. Two teenagers were standing about thirty feet in front of me, their faces covered and holding unlit Molotov cocktails. There were bricks and cinder blocks strewn across the road. I've learned that they will not harm regular civilians if they don't try to push past the roadblocks, so I turned around and went another way, along with the other cars. One of my boys talked about how their protest wasn't doing any good. I explained how it is hard to know for sure. I said they want to pressure the government and let them know they are not going away and sometimes pressure has to be exerted for a long time before change is noticeable.

I saw a video of a group of about thirty guys throwing Molotov cocktails at the police. I was surprised to see them standing in the midst of the tear gas, but then realized they were all wearing gas masks. This was the first time I had seen them actually in use against the police. One guy ran up to the police and fired something at them out of a fire extinguisher and then ran away.

30 OCTOBER 2012

@almayadeentv1

After 20 months of brutal crackdown and after MOI denied permission, huge turnout in AlEker #Bahrain http://twitpic.com/b87833 #سروري

Tarek Shalaby (@tarekshalaby)

#Bahrain News Agency | Interior Minister: All Rallies Are Banned until Security Is Maintained http://www.bna.bh/portal/en/news/531098#.UJAdbjPptEl.twitter …

AmnestyInternational (@AmnestyOnline)

Bahrain must lift ban on all protests http://ow.ly/eTdOn #humanrights @aibahrain

Micah Zenko (@MicahZenko)

Bahrain bans all public protests, claiming they're "A major threat to the safety of the public." http://on.ft.com/XSVnqq

Marc Owen Jones (@marcowenjones)

Arresting tweeps, blanket ban of protests, illegal to 'insult' the king. It is foolish to say that the uprising is over. #Bahrain

M. K. Al-Binateej (@ATEEKSTER)

It's about time such hate inciting violent protests were put to a stop. We've had enough of those who abuse #Bahrain freedoms

S.Yousif Almuhafda (@SAIDYOUSIF)

66% of expats either leaving or thinking about leaving #Bahrain mainly due to political instability http://goo.gl/HiXXu "

The government decided to ban all demonstrations in Bahrain. A couple of days ago, Al-Wefaq decided to proceed with a demonstration in Eker for which the government had denied approval. The Bahrain News Agency website reported the decision:

The Minister said because of such violations that risk civil peace and provoked anger among many members of Bahraini society that are fed up with those violations, there was a need to put an end to them.

The Interior Ministry has strived to tackle those violations through coordination with the organizers in many occasions, but they failed to control those events despite their promises," he added.

He said that it was decided to stop all rallies and gatherings until ensuring that security is maintained through achieving the targeted security to protect national unity and social fabric to fight extremism.

The Minister concluded that any illegal rally or gathering would be tackled through legal actions against those calling for it and participants, adding that anyone that would have a connection with such irregularities would be held accountable.

This will likely speed the country down the path of extremism. Now the more mainstream group Al-Wefaq will lose more followers to those who believe a peaceful path to reform no longer exists. It will probably also prompt the hard-line groups to adopt even more violent tactics. From social media, it is clear that every night there is demonstration activity in multiple places across the island. This decision was likely a result of pressure from the frustrated Sunni communities, who want the disruptions to stop. The problem is, if you don't give the people an avenue to vent their anger, it will manifest itself in more dangerous ways. It is clearer now more than ever that there is no way out of this without making some sort of deal.

The Eid Al-Adha holiday kept people home from work for a few days and perhaps contributed to a little more activity at night. A couple of nights ago, I was driving with my children to a friend's house in Karbabad, down Budaiyah Highway towards the Seef area. I saw cars braking, and then I saw the burning tires up ahead. I went off the road with a few other cars, and a guy got out of his car to move some cinder blocks that were blocking a narrow alleyway. After checking to make sure there wasn't anyone who might disapprove, I filed through and past the burning tires and back onto the road. At my friend's house, we barbequed some food while the children swam in the pool. We heard a couple of explosions, which I estimated to be about half a kilometer away. They were probably propane tanks, set off to provoke the police. Nobody said anything about it, just acknowledging the explosions with slight, unconcerned facial expressions.

31 OCTOBER 2012

Amber Lyon (@AmberLyon)
Four men in #Bahrain charged w/ "crime of insulting his majesty the king on Twitter" http://huff.to/Y11r0c

Mansoor Al-Jamri (@MANSOOR_ALJAMRi)
Guardian: "The situation is stagnant and there is no horizon for a political solution" said Mansoor al-Jamri #bahrain

http://m.guardian.co.uk/world/2012/oct/30/bahrain-opposition-protests-ban?cat=world&type=article …

Carlos Latuff (@CarlosLatuff)
When Hamad prohibits his people to protest in the streets it's because the streets don't belong to him anymore | #Bahrain

Kenneth Roth (@KenRoth)
Shunning US pressure for dialogue, #Bahrain tries pretending opposition has disappeared by banning public protests. http://trib.al/lCYze7

Ministry of Interior (@moi_bahrain)
Interior Minister: banning rallies & gatherings is a temporary decision until security is (cont) http://tl.gd/jrdj0t

At a Halloween party tonight, I talked to a Bahraini woman who said the major hurricane that hit the East Coast of the United States happened because of the anti-Islam movie that was made in America. She said something related to the production of the movie happened in New York. She said something else a group of people in America did (that is, a large group of naked people posing for a picture) caused the 9/11 terrorist attack. Then she said the reason the Shi'a have had such a hard time in many parts of the Middle East was because of how they treated Aisha, one of Mohammed's wives. It was the kind of conversation you just go along with. It made me think about how the Muslim world viewed their defeats in wars against Israel. After the 1967 war, many believed that they'd lost the war because they weren't practicing Islam faithfully enough, strengthening the fundamentalist movement.

Another Bahraini man talked about how the king is too timid to take decisive action and that the business community has had enough with the current situation and is demanding he fix things. He agreed that banning the protests was a token gesture, unlikely to improve the situation in any way. He then said that the unrest has led to a complete breakdown in the rule of law in their society. When people can throw Molotov cocktails and nothing happens to them, it is easy for people to think anything goes. You can see it on the streets the way people drive. He explained that before nobody had weapons, but now people are buying guns illegally for home protection.

5 NOVEMBER 2012

Sultan Sooud Al Qassemi @SultanAlQassemi
Bahrain activist in jail term for defaming King on Twitter http://goo.gl/VtZ3H | Detention of rights activist extended http://goo.gl/AknU6

Ministry of Interior (@moi_bahrain)
Two Asians dead, third seriously injured in five domestic terror explosions in Manama http://www.policemc.gov.bh/en/news_details.aspx?type=1&articleId=15289 …

Lucifer Arturo Ordog (@DeepDarkFear)
"We shall put explosives in garbage bins and harm innocent people because we want our FREEDOM!" - #Bahrain 'peaceful' protesters

Noor Turaif (@Noorealism)
What's up with this bomb news Bahrain?? That's terrorism not protest stop ruining the message and get your act together.

14 Feb Media Network (@Feb14Media)
#Bahrain #UN 4: Al-Wefaq: Truth behind incidents cannot be clearly detected due to absence of independent investigation... http://fb.me/1InwtJvYy

M. K. Al-Binateej (@ATEEKSTER)
If the garbage collector was a Shia Bahraini who died in a riot, Wefaq& their followers would condemn it on every channel & paper.

Early this morning a series of five bombs went off in the Adliya and Gudaibiya areas of Manama. Two South Asians were killed and another seriously wounded. There were five different devices. At least one was in a garbage dumpster that killed a street cleaner. Another bomb was outside a cinema, and another was on the sidewalk and went off when someone kicked the package or bag it was inside.

A lot of people are shocked and trying to figure out what this means. The deaths, and the fact that the explosions occurred on regular streets away from Shi'a neighborhoods or roadblocks, present a new dynamic. The indiscriminate nature of the attacks now puts everyone at risk when most people felt safe to be here. I had a few different people question me about whether they should proceed with their plans for the night. I expect the government is going to react with much less restraint. No group has claimed responsibility, and there is a sense on social media that this isn't helping the Shi'a cause. Perhaps it is in part a reaction to the government's ban on demonstrations.

This is a sad turn of events here, and I think this is a major setback for those calling for reforms. The government is much less likely to concede to any demands under these conditions. This could be the start of a much more dangerous phase of the unrest. I sincerely hope that those who did this see and feel the negative consequences of their actions and choose another path.

10 NOVEMBER 2012

Alwefaq Society (@ALWEFAQ)
http://alwefaq.net/index.php?show=news&action=article&id=7167
…Bahraini teen martyred after regime forces brutaaly attacked citizens heading to Friday prayer #bahrain

Ministry of Interior (@moi_bahrain)
After a burial in Samaheej, rioters blocked roads & committed acts of vandalism. Police restored order #Bahrain

المبرقعة Hind (@bahrainiac14)
I am in the martyr's funeral now with thousands of the angry Bahrainis chanting "down with king" #bahrain

Fawaz Al Khalifa (@fawaz_alkhalifa)

The national guard is patrolling areas around the car dealerships in sitra as a precautionary measure .. #bahrain

Mohammed Al-Maskati (@MohdMaskati)
Joint Statement: #Bahrain Authorities Withdraw Citizenship from 31 people, by Order of the King of Bahrain http://byshr.org/?p=1213 #BYSHR#BCHR

There have been a few other instances of pipe bombs going off, and almost every time I see people, they have another story of something they heard about. A few other pipe bombs in Gudaibiya are causing people to generally avoid the area until we see what happens next. The security guard where I live told me about how fifty-nine cars in a Sitra car dealership were burned. Others were worried about reports of a bomb going off in Sitra. A few believe Sunni extremists or the government placed the bombs, in an attempt to discredit the protesters, but I'm very skeptical of these theories. It is very likely a frustrated faction of the 14 February Movement.

As the Friday morning service began, about half of our church members still weren't there. I had received a few phone calls about all the roads being blocked, and it took one family two hours to make the twenty-minute drive. Apparently there were calls for all Shi'a to go to the mosque in Diraz to show their support for Isa Qassim. The government apparently didn't want a large gathering that could easily turn into a media spectacle, so they blocked all roads leading towards Diraz along the Budaiyah Highway. People tried walking there, and the police used tear gas and other means to stop them. There are conflicting reports, but some Shi'a say the boy who died was being chased by the police and was hit by a car. People seem worried that "it is happening again," referring to the chaos of last year.

The main English-language newspaper in Bahrain, which closely follows the government line, had a front page article alleging that Hezbollah and Iranian terrorists were coming to carry out attacks here. While it is hard to know the nature of their ties to outside groups, this information seems exaggerated and intended to justify a crackdown as well as an attempt to de-legitimize the opposition. The *Gulf Daily News* wrote:

The Lebanese militia had also deployed 300 to 400 of its agents to join other Iranian-linked terror cells in Bahrain, the Saudi Eastern Province, Kuwait and the UAE.

These agents have all been trained in intelligence operations, car bombings, planting deadly explosives in public and official places, in addition to assassinations.

14 NOVEMBER 2012

Ministry of Interior (@moi_bahrain)
Our countries expose to a colonial onslaught that uses the names of human rights, freedom or democracy

Manaf مـانـف (@Manafism)
"20% of #Bahrain population marched against regime..far greater than relative handful who mobilized in Tunisia & Egypt" http://goo.gl/PbGJC

Mohammed AlMaskati (@emoodz)
Footage of the National Guards aromred trucks seen around #Sitra yesterday, الأمور طيبة وإحنا بخير http://www.youtube.com/watch?v=Ejh4ZXc_9g8 … #Bahrain

ADHRB (@ADHRB)
@keithellison will encourage the #US to find other places to locate the #USFifthFleet. #Bahrain needs to comply w' int'l #HumanRights

I was driving on Khalifa bin Salman Highway, past the entrance to the Financial Harbor and the Souq, and I was very surprised to see an armored Humvee with a helmeted soldier positioned at the turret with a machine gun. The vehicle was in the area between the highways. I had seen media reports about National Guard vehicles on the streets to help the Ministry of Interior deal with the unrest. It is meant as a sign of resolve, but it also comes across as showing a degree of fear that things are out of control.

The usual activity continues every night with people starting to talk about how things are picking up again and making some comparisons to last year. In the news they are talking about how policemen are escorting the trash collectors after the pipe bombs that went off in Gudaibiya. The articles mentioned how many are afraid to do their jobs, and how they are being trained to do their work safely.

The Minister of Interior gave a speech at a joint GCC conference. I thought this statement said a lot: "Presently, our countries are exposed to a colonial onslaught that uses the pretext of human rights, freedom, or democracy to impose concepts of civilizations and cultures that are different from what we believe and want to protect."

Isa Qassim said this during his Friday sermon about the recent pipe bombs in Qudaibiya. Below is an English translation of part of that sermon, taken directly from Al-Wefaq's website:[xvi]

Expat targeting is a denounced crime and an outrageous oppression, it is religiously, rationally and consciously condemned and justified only by dirty political interests that take no considerations of religion, conscience and the nation interest.

Such an incident confirms the need for an impartial commission of inquiry as vital necessity to the general security situation.

Sixth: It is very clear that such crimes aim to push the situation towards violence and taking the country to the unknown situation. Therefore, the people must not respond to these Satanic aspirations that deepen the crisis and drown the country into distress and more painful circumstances.

20 NOVEMBER 2012

Chan'ad Bahraini (@chanadbh)
#PT So its okay to to use #Bahrain's biggest mosque for a pro-govt rally, but making a political statement in a Shia religious centre is not

Abu Al-Baik (@M_Ullah)
Meanwhile in Bahrain, an MP sets fire to an Israeli flag setting off the fire alarm... pic.twitter.com/Oi3fS7FY

IAA Bahrain (@IAA_Bahrain)
@moi_bahrain announced the arrest of number of persons suspected of involvement in arson of the Hyundai car warehouse 7/11/2012

Dominic Kavakeb (@DominicKavakeb)
Interesting that #bahrain govt has banned pro Palestinian protests over past few days.... #Gaza

Ministry of Interior (@moi_bahrain)
Recent meeting between Interior Minister &heads of Maatams & the summoning of some of them were within legal awareness to prevent violations

geety (@guityd)
#Bahrain just passed by Diraz few little boys holding flags near the round about aren't their parents worried?as a mother I would be worried

Things have been quieter the past few days, and people are saying it is because Shi'a are celebrating the upcoming Ashoura holiday. My wife was driving past Diraz village and saw a group of about twenty or thirty boys running around with flags. She said it didn't seem protest-related and probably had more to do with the religious holiday. There have been a number of protests commemorating a protestor who died last year.

This was on the MOI website: "The General Directorate of Crime Detection and Forensic Science has arrested a terror cell that placed fake bombs in several crowded areas throughout Bahrain. This included placing the objects on vital roads which caused traffic delays and spread fear among the public."

I was driving into Guraifa to get into Juffair tonight and was stopped at a police checkpoint. I was surprised that they stopped me, as I didn't realize what they wanted at first. I barely understood them say something about the US Navy. I said no, and after showing them my Bahraini ID card they let me pass easily, probably because of my Western appearance. I was pretty close to the US Navy base there. Maybe they were expecting some activity nearby?

25 NOVEMBER 2012

Mahmood Alshaikh (@M_Alshaikh)
#AP - A man covered in fake blood rides a horse in #Sanabis#Bahrain during a procession to mark #Ashura 24 11 12. http://twitpic.com/bg6eyg

Mohammed Ashoor (@mohdashoor)
Large pro-democracy anti-regime march on the streets of Sanabisnow. #Bahrain pic.twitter.com/v1s3NOkf

M. K. Al-Binateej (@ATEEKSTER)
During a Shia Ashoora ritual in Sanabis, some of the attacked police with Molotovs. Those who defend them are accomplices IMO.

Today is Ashoura. Ali gave me a call and told me I needed to go with him again to see the procession. I quickly made arrangements to leave work a little early and went home to change. Jeans and a black T-shirt helped me fit in much better than last year. They had the usual tables set up to hand out drinks and snacks, and everyone seemed in a happy and cooperative mood. Seeing two- or three-year-old boys on their fathers' shoulders, wearing the headbands we normally see Hezbollah or Hamas wear, is a reminder of how deep these feelings run.

I was moved again by the intensity of their marches and rituals. Perhaps the symbol of Hussein's martyrdom at Karbala will be the driving force behind their eventual success. Perceived injustice will drive many of them to action, even if success seems as elusive as ever.

The *Gulf Daily News* published these statistics today:[xvii]

EFFECTS of street violence since January this year:

10,934 illegal riots

456 policemen injured (56 with permanent disability)

129 police cars destroyed

614 civilian cars destroyed

505 minors involved in rioting or illegal demonstrations

7,356 instances of tyre burning to block main highways and further cripple the economy

1,470 vandalism cases reported by citizens

26 NOVEMBER 2012

Albahraini (@alhojairy)
Aftr 21months,ppl insist on reaching pearl roundabout; this is now aftr finishing relegious procession n Daih #bahrain

Mohammed Ashoor (@mohdashoor)
#Bahrain's police and paramilitary on high alert in and around Pearl Square as ppl gather for Ashoora procession in Daih village.

Mazen Mahdi (@MazenMahdi)
Heavy clashes in #Sanabis and #Daih following #Ashura march as mourners tried to reach #Lulu 1 confirmed arrest #Bahrain

We were pretty late to the Ashoura march yesterday, so Ali wanted us to go to the one in Daih today. He and his pregnant wife Fatima picked me up and after struggling to find parking, we walked into the area. We walked along with the marchers to get where we wanted to watch it, as Ali said hello to a few people and grabbed a drink for me. When it ended, nearly everyone started walking in the other direction. I thought they were just heading home, but soon I realized they were marching to the Pearl Roundabout. A little jokingly, I asked Fatima if she was going to retake the Pearl Roundabout with us. With a straight face, she said she would like to but is afraid of the tear gas, and she gestured to her baby.

We decided to go have a look from a distance, as she waited in the car for a few minutes. I could hear some loud booms that were probably sound or stun grenades. As we held back a little with a few hundred others, I noticed that none of the guys wearing headbands stopped, but instead they kept marching all the way to the front. I could see clouds of tear gas down the road, and then suddenly everyone started running in the other direction, that is, towards us. We quickly walked to the car as Ali told me to hurry, even though I didn't really see any danger.

As we slowly made our way out, people were running past us. A few fathers were jogging along with infants in their arms and quickly put them in a car. A group of young men turned to hear someone warning about the police, and everyone quickly cleared out of the area.

A few seconds later, a group of about sixty riot police marched past us, down the narrow road, wearing helmets and body armor and carrying shields and batons. A couple of them had video cameras. I wanted to take a picture of the police but when I asked, Ali and Fatima urgently told me not to. They said if I did, the police would break the car windows, destroy the camera, and arrest us. Fatima was worried about breathing any tear gas and kept asking Ali if he smelt any. Later that night, I drove past the Seef area, where the Pearl Roundabout is, and saw about twenty riot police vehicles, and over a hundred policemen waiting to defend the area.

2 DECEMBER 2012

Breaking News (@BreakingNews)
Riot police fired tear gas to disperse more than 50 hardline Islamic protesters denouncing Kim Kardashian's presence in Bahrain - @AP

Kim Kardashian (@KimKardashian)
Thanks Sheikh Khalifa for your amazing hospitality. I'm in love with The Kingdom of Bahrain @bu_daij70

AlwefaqEN (@AlWefaqEN)
AlWefaq: The regime in #Bahrain destroys mosques again today 1Dec 2012 part of its war on religious freedoms.pic.twitter.com/EI7APgn0

السلمان ميثم (@MaythamAlsalman)
The Govt. of #Bahrain once again demolishes "Al Imam Al Hassan Al Askari mosque" in Hamad Town today. #Islam

Agence France-Presse (@AFP)
Bahraini police have fired tear gas to break up protests overnight in Shiite-populated villages around Manama http://bit.ly/TzdHTz

Since the end of the Ashoura celebrations, the demonstration activity has really picked up. Every night for the past few days, there have been tire-burnings, small protests in several villages, and attacks on police.

One evening, I was hurrying home from work to arrive before my wife had to leave. Up ahead, on the main highway leading towards the Saudi Causeway, I saw police headlights, and cars putting their hazard lights on, as they often do when they are slowing down. It was quickly apparent that the police were shutting down the highway and diverting us to another exit. I could see other traffic stopped far up ahead and knew what it was—likely a fake bomb near a burning roadblock. I took a number of back roads and got back on the highway via another entrance. I could see the traffic was still blocked further back, and I was one of the only cars on the highway.

On my wife's way home tonight she stopped off in a Shi'a village to talk to a *shwarma* guy she had been referred to by a friend about making shwarmas for a Christmas party. She said as she negotiated on the street, there was a growing crowd interested in the odd scene of a blonde-haired lady in their village, apparently working out some big deal. On the way home, she said there were about twelve police SUVs outside the village of Diraz, where Sheikh Isa Qassim lives.

10 DECEMBER 2012

Volker Perthes (@volkerperthes)
Mass rally in #Bahrain. Ali Salman calls for peacefulness and democratic state; demonstartors chant: we don't kneel except for God.

Maryam Alkhawaja (@MARYAMALKHAWAJA)
what cp of #bahrain did best: talk about beautiful ideas of democracy and reforms, while ignoring daily human rights violations #IISS_ME

Mazen Mahdi (@MazenMahdi)
RT @ElaineMasons: Inside the Car where Young Aqeel was Shot in the Face. pic.twitter.com/OnWtLqXA #bahrain

There are numerous posts and graphic photos of a young man who was shot in the face with bird shot. Some reports say he intentionally tried to run through a police roadblock. He is in Salmaniya Hospital, and there have been numerous demonstrations protesting the attack.

At an international security conference held in Bahrain over the past few days, called the Manama Dialogue, the crown prince gave a speech where he called for dialogue. The main political societies accepted his invitation. He said:

Geopolitically, demographically, and historically the differing political views represented in disparate political groups in Bahrain must be reconciled, and they will only by reconciled by sitting together and agreeing a framework where the limit of what is acceptable is the limit of what is unacceptable to the other with the ultimate goal being to reach an agreement.

I am not a prince of Sunni Bahrain, I am not a prince of Shi'a Bahrain, I am a prince of the Kingdom of Bahrain and all mean a great deal to me personally. And I soon hope to see a meeting between all sides, and I call for a meeting between all sides, as I believe that only through face-to-face contact will any real progress be made.

I drove through Saar tonight on my way to a friend's house, and I ended up going a different way and got a little lost. There were several roads that were completely blocked up with trash, wood, cinder blocks, and other materials. Other roads were almost blocked, leaving only a narrow opening for one car to get through, but with other items placed nearby to close it off when necessary. I saw a video clip of police in Bilad al-Qadeem rapidly firing well over a hundred tear gas canisters in all directions, causing a thick cloud to blanket the area. Even though it didn't show if anything had provoked the action, it didn't appear to be dealing with a threat to their safety. The protest activity has really picked up this past week, but people think it may pick up even more as the holy month of Muharram ends, and as we approach the sixteenth, Bahrain's National Day.

18 DECEMBER 2012

Nicholas Kristof (@NickKristof)
@AsalBarak I denounced oppression in Iran, as I do in Bahrain, as I do in Gitmo. Iran & Bahrain agree on 1 thing: they don't like my reports

Mohamed Hasan (@safybh)
On this day 1994 two young men were killed in #BAHRAIN marking this day as the martyrs day, in 2010 it became the start of arab revolutions

ArabianBusiness.com (@ArabianBusiness)
Bahrain breaks up protests, arrests campaigner: Bahraini police fired stun grenades to break up dozens of protes... http://bit.ly/ZHdke3

On my way to work on December 11, at around 7.30 in the morning, traffic was really backed up near Tubli. I saw a helicopter overhead and found out later that tires had been lit across the highway around 7:00 a.m.

Bahrain celebrated National Day on 16 and 17 December. There are red and white lights up all around the country. They celebrate it in part to commemorate the king's ascension to the throne. Many Shi'a have dubbed it Martyr's Day and have planned a large protest in Manama. The police blocked many of the roads leading into the area. The Shi'a protestors planned smaller demonstrations surrounding the Souq area, and then all marched into the area. The police used tear gas and stun grenades and arrested several people. I talked to some people about what they should do to avoid the expected activity and whether it was safe to go into certain areas. Since Muharram ended, there has been protests and related street violence in Shi'a neighborhoods across Bahrain. Things should kick up again during the GCC summit to be held in Bahrain next week. I saw in the paper that some people threw Molotov cocktails at a restaurant in Jidh Ali. Assuming that it was a form of attempted Shi'a protest activity, I hope wiser heads will prevail, seeing that this kind of action does not further their cause and only strengthens the government's narrative against them.

31 DECEMBER 2012

The Observers (@observers)
The police slap heard all over Bahrain | The Observers

Kristian Ulrichsen (@Dr_Ulrichsen)
Video of policeman in #Bahrain slapping a young father holding his baby continues to go viral, more than 424,000 views

Ministry of Interior (@moi_bahrain)
A policeman was ran over by a car intentionally in Sanabis. Police launched investigation #Bahrain

دي فيفدي سون كري ستوفر [Christopher Davidson] (@dr_davidson)
As #GCC summit takes place in #Bahrain, ministers must be conscious that with Syria in the endgame, the winds are ready to blow south.

Two officers from the Bahrain National Security Agency were sentenced to seven years in prison. Abdulkarim Fakhrawi, a prominent businessman, died in government custody last April. According to the *Gulf Daily News*, "They (the defendants) grabbed the toilet seat from the victim's hand, pushed him to the ground and continuously hit him. He (the victim) lost balance and the officers started to kick him on his sides and one of the agents hit him with the toilet seat. After he fell and stopped resisting, they continued to beat him up in revenge." There is some feeling of justice by the Shi'a, but to many people, seven years seems too short a sentence.

A video of a policeman slapping a man holding a baby has caused quite a stir. The man didn't have any identification with him, and the policeman slapped him while questioning him about where he lived. Many comments have tried to paint this as typical of the regime and further evidence of its despicable nature. The police said the officer was tried in secret and convicted. These are the type of things that can be turning points in the rise and fall of the unrest here.

The GCC summit, which is being held in Bahrain from 23-25 December, announced a decision to form a unified GCC military command structure. They warned Iran to stop meddling in their internal affairs. Oppositionists pointed out the irony of the government hosting the summit and being critical of Assad, when in their minds Bahrain is not that far from being like Syria.

I was in Oman last week and a rental car attendant starting talking about how all religions are so similar and how people shouldn't make such a big deal about different sects, such as Sunni and Shi'a. He asked about how things were in Bahrain and I told him that every day there were people burning tires to block the roads and frequently there were Molotov cocktail attacks against the police. He seemed genuinely disappointed and didn't see any justification for their protests.

This last week there have been daily protests in a variety of Shi'a areas, including tire-burnings and propane-tank explosions. Many of them seem to be coordinated to occur at the same time of day. There are some comments about the protestors trying to prepare the way for more aggressive activity on New Year's Day.

6 JANUARY 2013

Jasmin Ali (@Jasmin5505)
Winning is already a great feeling but beating #saudi makes it even better #Iraq #iraqsoccer

Zeinab (@xxo_Zeinab_oox)
IRAQ is the best they aint terrorists they good soccer players !!!! KSA go home yall got nothin to do

Dr Ala'a Shehabi (@alaashehabi)
View the meticulous documentation of 221 instances of access denial into #Bahrain here http://bahrainwatch.org/access/data.php TRUE FIGURES R MUCH HIGHER

الإخبارية لمدمر ش. (@ModmorNews)
#UN #UK #SOS #USA MN.3#Bahrain | #Sitra : violent clashes in Sitra at the night of symbols leaders' trial http://fb.me/1BpgagFLJ

Liz_Lane (@Elish_Neline)

#Bahrain #UK #USA #IrelandTonight police and motorists get caught in a Molotov attack by Alwefaq terrorists http://fb.me/HLs9JH2E

Tonight two of my children and I went to the Iraq-Saudi Arabia football match. As we walked toward the stadium, we were excited when a guy handed us tickets. We soon found out the tickets were meaningless, as they had stopped letting people in. Every few minutes, stadium officials would let one person in, causing a crush of young men to fight towards the front of the turnstile. We finally made our way to the front, but by the time we got there, they had stopped letting people in altogether. I realized that there was extra interest in this game. There were all types of police and security there, but the crowd seemed strangely similar to what you'd see at sporting events in Europe. When we heard Iraq score a goal, we saw a lot of people outside celebrating. I suspected that the Shi'a in Bahrain were probably supporting Iraq against the Saudis, which I later heard was the case. Some guys made a halfhearted effort to climb over the fence, but everyone seemed to respect the security forces enough to not try it. We sat in a cafe eating ice cream, near a group of serious and unhappy looking Saudis. Guys were standing out of their sunroofs, waving the Iraqi flags, and yelling at Saudis walking by, who just smiled a little.

There was a lot of talk of protestors trying to disrupt the Gulf Cup football tournament that goes through the eighteenth. So far there hasn't been much more than the usual activity in the usual places. Perhaps there is some hesitation, worrying that disrupting this event wouldn't really bring the right kind of attention or sympathy to their cause. I suspect they will make a big statement in some way. Maybe they can relate to football matches more than events like the Formula One and Jewelry Expositions.

The Pakistani embassy said Pakistanis in Bahrain have been fearing for their lives following the attack on Tasleem Gul Khan on Monday. The twenty-three-year-old victim was guarding a water pump at a construction company worksite in Sitra, when three men confronted him and poured flammable liquid on him before setting him on fire. The Pakistani embassy had recorded nearly 2,000 cases of their nationals attacked by anti-government protesters during the 2011 unrest, including some who suffered from serious injuries. I've heard people say the attacks are because some Shi'a resent the Pakistanis who are working in the Bahrain police force, and they take it out on other Pakistani residents.

JANUARY 13, 2013

Durazy (@Durazy)
RED: the blood of angry men .... BLACK: the color of the ages passed ... #les_miserables #bahrain #bh_revolution

The Daily Star (@DailyStarLeb)
Bahrain Shiites protest at jail for 13 activists: Thousands of Shiites demonstrate near Manama in a new protest ...http://bit.ly/ZTWQQf

AlwefaqEN (@AlWefaqEN)
Today 3:30 #Bahrain masses will march streets to demand #democracy and release of prisoners of conscience unfairly given lenghtly sentences

Mona Kareem (@monakareem)
LOL King of #Bahrain won the title of the Humanitarian Personality of the Year by a kuwaiti newspaper that no one reads

On my way into work this morning, I saw a police helicopter fly low over the highway near Al-Wefaq headquarters, which is situated near Bilad al-Qadeem and Tubli. The government authorized an Al-Wefaq demonstration to take place on Friday on Budaiyah Highway, the first one I recall them authorizing since they banned demonstrations altogether earlier this year. Many other smaller demonstrations occur in the Shi'a villages, sometimes leading to confrontations with the police. The nightly activity continues, but rarely disrupting activity outside Shi'a areas.

I saw the movie *Les Miserables* at the Saar Cinema last night. As we drove to the theater, at the main intersection leading into the village where there are frequently roadblocks, I saw five police SUVs parked with policeman standing outside their vehicles. I've heard people call that intersection "Barbeque Ally" because of how frequently there are burning roadblocks, and because of all the black ash scattered around. As I watched the movie, I wondered how much Shi'a in Bahrain would draw inspiration from the story and was surprised government screeners allowed it to be shown.

20 JANUARY 2013

Sayed Hassan (@WLEXT)
AP named yesterdays protests "street clashes"!! security forces fired tear gas & protesters fired slogans?

jassim alrowaie (@kingjr222)
Batelco services hit after arson attack in Sitra http://www.gulf-daily-news.com/NewsDetails.aspx?storyid=345851 … #Bahrain #Terrorism

AlwefaqEN (@AlWefaqEN)
Citizens marched #Bahrain Capital yesterday demanding#democracy but were faced with regime's toxic gas and birdshot

The Gulf Cup football tournament ended a couple days ago. There wasn't as much protest activity as people expected, although after a victory you would see fans celebrating by driving around in their cars, with their heads out of the window, waving flags. Before the final match between UAE and Iraq, I saw my Shi'a friend Ali at an intersection. I asked if he had seen any matches, and he said no, and that he wasn't interested in football and was happy Bahrain was out of it. He then gave me a thumbs-up about Iraq being in the final. I suppose some people still identify the national team of Bahrain with the ruling family.

I had to resolve an issue with the bus driver who picks people up for church. A new family lives in a predominately Shi'a neighborhood, and the bus driver said he didn't want to go in there to pick them up. I explained that things are usually calm on Friday morning, but he insisted that it wasn't a place he should be going. I arranged for him to pick them up at a store on a major road near their home, so he would not have to go inside the neighborhood.

Protest activity is picking up this week, likely as people are getting excited about the 14 February anniversary of the unrest. Some of the activity seems to be happening outside the Shi'a neighborhoods, as I've heard about burning roadblocks placed in Exhibition Road and Al-Fateh Highway. An English lady we talked to at the National Theater last night said it had been quiet lately, but that the other night she heard what sounded like repeated gunshot exchanges outside her home in Saar.

For the first time, I drove down a road that runs along the northern coast, through a number of Shi'a neighborhoods. There were a few spots where the road was blocked, leaving only a narrow lane open. There were logs and other debris piled to one side, so people could seal it off quickly if needed. There were a lot of remnants of burned material in some areas. Nobody seemed to pay me any special attention, except for possibly a car with some young guys that was stopped on the side of the road. When I passed, they pulled out behind me and followed me for about a kilometer before turning.

25 JANUARY 2013

Mohammed aKa Big Mo (@ba7rainiDXB)
Limited access to #Manama has begun ID's checked and only residents are allowed in. No demonstrations allowed #Bahrainpic twitter.com/y1aCHxQ3

rick (@rickrick888)
Protests erupt in Bahrain capital: Tear gas and stun grenades are fired by police against anti-government protesters... http://dlvr.it/2rb5LN

Reem Khalifa (@Reem_Khalifa)
BBC News - Bahraini opposition accepts talks offer to end crisis http://bbc.in/XU4PZg #Bahrain #14Feb

M. K. Al-Binateej (@ATEEKSTER)
Video: killing of the #Bahrain policeman (Muraisi) The killer got the death sentence & his accomplice got life https://www.youtube.com/watch?v=f8vgwnvttuU&feature=youtube_gdata_player ...

A few days ago I was driving through Juffair and saw a dump truck full of tires with a few police vehicles surrounding it. I found out later online that they had seized the tires during raids they had conducted in the area. This week, driving down a main highway on my way home from work, I saw what appeared to be a house on fire about a half a kilometer in the distance. Another time there was light smoke across the road and surrounding areas but I couldn't tell where it was coming from.

Last night as my wife was driving to meet me and some of our friends in the Seef area, she got lost. She was in Manama somewhere, but I had no way of helping her as nothing she described sounded familiar. She drove into some areas she knew she shouldn't be in, as she was getting strange looks, with one young kid even pointing at her.

At the roundabout near the International Hospital of Bahrain, she came across a burning roadblock that had died down, but was still burning. She said as she passed through it, she just wondered casually how she could get through it with the least amount of damage to her tires. She realized later just how much more casual she is about experiencing things like that.

1 FEBRUARY 2013

الرساس ناصر (@NaserAlRess)
#Bahrain has fallen 66 places in the space of four years and is now in the bottom 20, PRESS FREEDOM INDEX 2013 http://en.rsf.org/press-freedom-index-2013,1054.html …

Brian Dooley (@dooley_dooley)
Al Wefaq leader Ali Salman: if jailed #Bahrain leaders not in the dialogue "the dialogue will fail" http://m.bbc.co.uk/news/world-middle-east-21267591 …@amanialmasqati

AlwefaqEN (@AlWefaqEN)
Ahmed Qattan,16 another victim of #Bahrain regime, was killed with birdshot, an internationally banned weapon @UNICEFt.co/VcbZ6OWM

Ministry of Interior (@moi_bahrain)
After the end of a funeral in Diah, rioters blocked roads & committed acts of vandalism. Police restored order #Bahrain

Saw-saw-sa-san (@SawsanKhanum)
We got attacked, same toxic gas that killed the 8y/o martyr Qassim shot at people marching after his funeral #Bahrain

Hassiba HadjSahraoui (@HassibaHS)
#Bahrain's authorities insist on 5 day limit on Int'l NGO visits limiting our ability to independtly investigate human rights abuses

Ministry of Interior (@moi_bahrain)
Three policemen sustained minor injuries in a terror attack by remotely detonate homemade bomb at Jid Hafs roundabout in Budaiya #Bahrain

Ministry of Interior (@moi_bahrain)
4 policemen sustained minor injuries in a blast of a homemade bombin Bilad Al Qadeem #Bahrain

A lot happened this week. Both sides debated whether an eight-year-old boy had died from tear gas, or from natural causes. Then of course they both disagreed on whether the police attacked the funeral mourners, or whether the funeral mourners marched towards the police and provoked them. A bomb went off two days ago in Jidh Hafs, near the International Hospital, and wounded some police officers. According to social media, more policemen were injured by a bomb tonight. Police were responding to burning tires on the road when the device exploded.

There was a little extra security at the Seef Mall when we went there, and they seemed a little more prepared to act. A friend mentioned his child's tennis practice had been canceled twice in a row because of tear gas coming through the fences. I read about things happening every night. I saw one video where a group of about forty people attacked one police car with Molotov cocktails. Somehow when it was over, the car pulled away. I happened to drive through a neighborhood near Sitra the other day, and every road in the area had barricades set up with trees, cinder blocks, and other items that allowed just a single car to pass through. People are starting to ask again: what is going to happen this 14 February? Most likely, the street violence will increase in intensity, and probably there will be more of these small bombs we are starting to see. Several thousand will probably march towards the old Pearl Roundabout again as a symbolic act, to keep their cause alive, even if they know they won't actually reoccupy the area, as the police have the force to stop them. I'm not sure what effect the bombs will have on the police if this trend continues.

8 FEBRUARY 2013

Anmar Kamalaldin (@anmarek)
Flags of #Bahrain flying at pro-democracy rally organised by 5 opposition societies pic.twitter.com/GixL5HSc

Agence France-Presse (@AFP)
Bahrain's national dialogue resumes Sunday in atmosphere of mistrust between government & opposition: http://bit.ly/XYS7WJ by

Zaid Benjamin (@zaidbenjamin)
#Bahrain Justice Minister says the national dialogue will be launched on Sunday and the agenda will be agreed upon in the first session

Shashank Joshi (@shashj)
"Iran is engaged in a proxy struggle with Saudi Arabia and other Gulf states in Bahrain" https://csis.org/files/publication/TWQ_13Winter_Flanagan.pdf … No evidence for that, but OK.

Abu Saber (@Moawen)
Weekdays or weekends, thousands are protesting in #Bahrain daily in the 2nd anniversary of the uprising https://www.youtube.com/watch?

M. K. Al-Binateej (@ATEEKSTER)
Don't you dare bring your stinky filth on this island. If you burn tires here in Muharraq then accept any consequences! #Bahrain

Both sides seem to be gearing up for next week's 14 February anniversary of the unrest in Bahrain. Tonight I was driving along Khalifa bin Salman Highway near the Burgerland Roundabout and I saw truck carrying very large cement barriers followed by a bulldozer and several police vehicles with their lights on. They were likely on their way to set up a barricade somewhere, possibly a new checkpoint. At the exit to the Adhari Park gas station, there were additional armored vehicles and what appeared to be a large police armored water truck. I see remnants of burned tires every couple of days and I hear the demonstrations are happening more frequently across the island.

The government has arranged for a dialogue with the opposition political "societies" to begin on 10 February 2013. It was a very shrewd move on the government to begin the talk a few days before the anniversary. It will put pressure on the opposition to moderate their support for aggressive action and is close enough that it likely won't fail or fall apart before the anniversary comes.

Syria seems to be weighing on a lot of people's minds here, especially about what it means for reform in Bahrain. Both sides accuse the other of hypocrisy as the Shi'a tend to support the Assad dictatorship, and the Sunnis in general—and the Bahraini government specifically—support its overthrow. I've even heard some talk of how some Shi'a are viewing this as another sign of impending return of the Mahdi. A recent Carnegie Endowment for International Peace study stated, "But the status quo is not sustainable indefinitely. With the likely fall of the Alawite-dominated government in Syria, Bahrain's Al Khalifa family will soon be the only sectarian minority in the Middle East ruling over a majority that has little-to-no say in its government. Recent history suggests that, absent sweeping structural changes, the outcome for such an arrangement will not be peaceful."[xviii]

13 FEBRUARY 2013

nazihasaeed (@nazihasaeed)
For the Valentine #MoI decided to put on the street a policeman for each citizen #BAHRAIN

Ma'an News Agency (@MaanNewsAgency)
#mideast Bahrain Air closes down, blames political unrest http://bit.ly/12tLoY5

Salman Shaikh (@Salman_Shaikh1)
Oh dear .... "@Naharnet: #Breaking Al-Arabiya: A bomb exploded in a shopping mall in the city of Issa in Bahrain. http://www.naharnet.com/ "

Ministry of Interior (@moi_bahrain)
A domestic terror act of remotely detonate explosion targeted lives at a shopping center in Isa Town that led to limited damages #Bahrain

Ahmed Al-haddad (@AhmdHaddad)
14FEB COALITION calls for a march Friday 15-02-2013, towards Pearl Roundabout that is imposed to security cordon since two years. #Bahrain

Yesterday a minor explosion occurred inside the Ramez Shopping Centre in Isa Town, a predominantly Sunni area. From the looks of the photo, it appeared to only have knocked some things off a shelf. Nobody was injured, but it really had an impact on people. These types of incidents really change how secure people feel, as their world and safety seem really unpredictable. If there are more attacks that seem to be intentionally planned to occur in Sunni areas, this will definitely lead to negative sectarian tensions, making it even less likely that the protestors will obtain the rights they are hoping for.

Yesterday on my way home, it seemed everywhere I looked I could see the blue flashing lights of police vehicles. Tonight I saw a long convoy of about eight dark blue armored vehicles of a few different varieties, and about ten police SUVs. They were heading towards the Budaiyah Highway area. This past week the protest activity has dramatically increased. Tomorrow is the second anniversary of the uprising and there have been plenty of warnings to keep travel limited.

I was driving on Budaiyah Highway tonight, past the village of Diraz. Up ahead of me, I saw a fire on the road, and then could see that it had just been lit and there were a few people still standing on the road. One guy raised his arm high in the air with something on fire in his hand and held it there for a couple of seconds. It was not a threatening pose but a statement of defiance. After a moment they ran off, and the cars slowly moved by.

The government initiated what they are describing as a "National Dialogue" between the government and several of the larger political "societies" in Bahrain. They are meeting twice a day and the largest Shi'a group, Al-Wefaq, seems to be cautiously going along for now. I am confident the government is not prepared to make the concessions necessary to end the conflict. I worry that the longer they wait, the more polarized both sides will be.

14 FEBRUARY 2013

Nicholas Kristof (@NickKristof)
On 2nd anniversary of #Bahrain protests, more violence & a teenage protester reported shot dead. Both sides polarized.

Yacoub Al-Slaise (@yslaise)
In #Bahrain, going on general strike means terrorizing your neighbours, burning veg/fruit stalls, blocking roads and assaulting ppl+property

Brian Dooley (@dooley_dooley)
Not even 7am in #Bahrain and reports of protests in many parts of the country, inc Duraz. al Eker, Bilad al Qadeem, Aali & Bani Jamrah

Today is the day. It started with tire burnings on the major highways, causing severe traffic problems in some areas. I heard there were relatively large gatherings in many different neighborhoods. I saw a burned out propane tank that had been detonated since last night. One young man died from a shotgun wound. The police said they were defending themselves as he was throwing a Molotov cocktail at them.

I drove through Sitra, Saar, and Budaiyah Highway this afternoon. The police were out in large numbers in many different areas. Nearly all of the side streets had roadblocks set up. Some had narrow paths left clear, while others were completely blocked with large trees, stones, or other objects. Trash dumpsters, bricks, and other items, including a couple of bathtubs and a toilet, were strewn across several different roads. I saw one young man, who had his face covered with a shirt, pulling things onto a road. Some of the roadblocks were on fire, and I saw tear gas clouding a street between the police and some protesters in Sitra. In several other areas I saw smoke rising in the distance.

Tonight on my way home I drove past the old Pearl Roundabout. Police were out in riot gear with helmets and shields. Going down Budaiyah Highway, I saw some very large cement blocks placed on the road near the Country Mall. About fifteen police cars were in the area. Some vehicles were partially up on the curb, having apparently only recently arrived, as some of the police officers were still getting out of their cars, and all were looking out into the dark, tree-covered area. A little further down, I saw police moving cinder blocks from a side road as several other policemen kept watch in case of trouble. Diraz and other areas had about fifteen police SUVs and a couple armored vehicles with ten to twenty officers standing looking into the roads entering the village. When I passed Bani Jamra, I saw about thirty police officers and about five of them were firing tear gas into the village. I could see several blocked roads heading inside the area. Closer to Janabiyah, I saw both sides of the road blocked with burning tires and the police on the scene were trying to figure out what to do about the other side. My side had already been cleared and the other side was cleared enough to let one lane pass by slowly. Just now I heard an explosion in the distance that sounded like thunder, most likely a propane tank. Other people who avoided these and other common demonstration areas might have only seen the traffic this morning and possibly some smoke in the distance.

15 FEBRUARY 2013

Ministry of Interior (@moi_bahrain)
4 arrested and with them ammunitions they used in the shooting at the police in Karzakan, search continues for the rest #Bahrain

Gregg Carlstrom (@glcarlstrom)
Bahraini interior ministry says a police officer was killed by a fire-bomb during overnight clashes: http://bit.ly/12QGSaF

Ahmed Al-haddad (@AhmdHaddad)
Teargassed, the street thats few min away from Pearl Rounabout. pic. twitter.com/19d8bK6f You can see LULU TOWERS #Bahrain

Mahmood Alshaikh (@M_Alshaikh)
#AP - An anti-government Protesters wearing national flags and a scarf that reads, "ready to die for #Bahrain" http://twitpic.com/c45gc4

On my way in this morning, on the highway just after you enter Bahrain from Saudi Arabia, I saw a new billboard advertising the Bruce Willis movie, *A Good Day to Die Hard.* In light of all the talk about death and martyrs for the cause, and the expected attempts to march again towards the old Pearl Roundabout area, I found it an odd coincidence. Perhaps Shi'a will view it as similar to Hussein and his attempt to go to Karbala. He persisted even though he was outnumbered, because his sense of justice required it. I suspect nearly all Shi'a know they are not going to re-occupy the area by marching there, due to the overwhelming police presence, but as a symbol of their cause, they feel like they have to make the attempt.

Things were very active again in many areas of Bahrain: skirmishes, street battles, things burning, tear gas, stun grenades, road blocks, Molotov cocktails, demonstrations both small and large. About half the people in our church stayed home today because of the unrest. I knew there was going to be a large march today along Budaiyah Highway and many people expected part of the group to go to the Pearl. When I drove over Budaiyah Highway, the traffic was moving slowly. The Burgerland Roundabout was closed, and there were a few hundred policemen and dozens of police vehicles staged to stop the advance towards the Pearl. From the overpass, I could see a wall of tear gas about four hundred meters away that was effective in keeping the crowd from moving forward.

I drove into Saar (not far from where the march had taken place). Traffic was moving very slowly and a bit chaotically as cars moved to fill in any gap they could find. I saw hundreds, maybe thousands of people walking back to their cars. Many of the men were wearing black, like they did during Ashoura. Helicopters flew overhead. The photos of the march showed tens of thousands of people marching in all four lanes.

One policeman was killed by an explosion and other policemen received shotgun wounds. The violent oppositionists are getting more effective, and this is the first instance I've heard of them using live ammunition rather than their makeshift devices. Overall, things were similar to last year, but the tactics have become more lethal. Unfortunately, this is the trend we are on, with no break in sight.

FINAL THOUGHTS

Would the almost universally accepted virtue of democracy let us down? Does democracy always lead to a better place? The track record is pretty good, but there have been exceptions. The Arab Spring, the election of Hamas, and the new government in Iraq all raise serious questions about whether popular movements controlled by certain Islamist strains can really better serve the interests of their people. The Bahraini government should make a deal now while they can still preserve their interests and role in the future government. Time isn't on their side. Businesses will continue to leave. The government's frustration will continue, and they will take it out on the protestors. The Sunni community will increasingly pressure the government to bring things back to the way they were. They will alienate even more people, to the point where calls for an end to the regime might become even more widely accepted and deeply held.

Legitimacy is granted by the people. The Al Khalifa government needs to do what it needs to do in order to get that legitimacy back while they still can. They haven't done a bad job running the country. Many of the grievances the Shi'a have against the Khalifa government really aren't sufficient cause in the minds of most outsiders to justify an end to their rule. However, the current government structure does seem inequitable on the surface—Uncle Khalifa being the prime minister for the last forty years, for example—and the winds of the

Arab Spring may fade periodically, but they won't go away here. The Khalifas are not dictators on the scale of Assad and Gaddafi. In fact, before the Arab Spring, Bahrain was frequently praised as a leading political reformer in the region. Even so, the social contract has been broken, and they need to repair it. Clearing the burning tires every night, regularly dispersing "unauthorized" demonstrations with riot control agents, and sacrificing their police officers to the Molotov cocktails and other projectiles of the demonstrators, is not going to get it done.

The protestors are most likely to have success in their future if they pursue a peaceful path. They largely have the support of the international media. If they tarnish their cause with violence, it will justify the heavy government response, and this will turn into a bloody sectarian conflict that may not end in their favor—with a bridge connected to Saudi Arabia. As civil rights movements throughout the last century have shown, consistent pressure is more likely to sway people than bombs and guns. Let's hope that if they pursue this path, and succeed in getting the representation they are looking for, they will maintain the culturally vibrant and tolerant society that is part of why so many people love Bahrain.

NOTES

[i]   Heinz Halm. *Shi'ism*. (New York: Columbia University Press, 2004), 85.

[ii]   Graham Fuller and Rend Rahim Francke. *The Arab Shi'a: The Forgotten Muslims*. (New York: St. Martin's Press, 1999), 121.

[iii]   Halm, 132.

[iv]   John Duke Anthony. *Arab States of the Lower Arabian Gulf: People, Politics, Petroleum*. (Washington D.C.: Middle East Institute, Capital City Press, 1975), 46.

[v]   Fuad I. Khuri. *Tribe and State in Bahrain: The Transformation of Social and Political Authority in an Arab State*. (Chicago: University of Chicago Press, 1980), 195.

[vi]   Anthony, 47.

[vii]   Anthony, 48.

[viii] Anthony, 49.

[ix] Anthony, 64.

[x] Anthony, 49.

[xi] Anthony, 51.

[xii] Emile A Nakhleh. *Bahrain: Political Development in a Modernizing Society.* (Lexington, Massachusetts, D.C. Heath and Co., 1976), 153–155.

[xiii] Caversham BBC, "Guide to Bahraini parliamentary election, 25 November 2006," 10 Nov 2006.

[xiv] Frederic Wheyrey. *The Precarious Alley: Bahrain's Impasse and US Policy.* Carnegie Endowment for International Peace, 06 February 2013.

[xv] http://www.alwefaq.org/index_lite.php?show=news&action=download&id=7083

[xvi] http://alwefaq.net/index_lite.php?show=news&action=download&id=7180

[xvii] http://www.gulf-daily-news.com/NewsDetails.aspx?storyid=342297

[xviii] Frederic Wheyrey. *The Precarious Alley: Bahrain's Impasse and US Policy.* Carnegie Endowment for International Peace, 06 February 2013.